VAULTING

VAULTING

The Art of Gymnastics on the Moving Horse

By ELIZABETH FRIEDLAENDER

THE STEPHEN GREENE PRESS

BRATTLEBORO, VERMONT

Rock Valley College
Educational Resources
Center

Copyright© 1970 by Elizabeth Friedlaender. All rights reserved. No part of this book may be reproduced without written permission from the publisher, except by a reviewer who may quote brief passages or reproduce illustrations in a review; nor may any part of this book be reproduced, stored in a retrieval system or transmitted in any form or by any means electronic, mechanical, photocopying, recording, or other, without written permission from the publisher.

This book has been manufactured in the United States of America; designed by R. L. Dothard, set in type by Mono Typesetting, printed and bound by Halliday Lithograph Corporation. It is published by The Stephen Greene Press, Brattleboro, Vermont 05301.

Library of Congress Catalog Card Number: 72-118228
International Standard Book Number: 0-8289-0122-8

Contents

FOREWORD 7

INTRODUCTION 9

PREPARATION 11

BUILDING THE FOUNDATION 27

ADVANCED WORK FOR VAULTING TEAMS 53

EXHIBITIONS 86

COMPETITIONS 91

GLOSSARY AND INDEX 101

APPENDIX 112

SCORING CHARTS 116

Acknowledgments

The writer does not claim to be an authority on the subject of vaulting. Rather, she is one who has found in it a delightful adjunct to the riding program for children and wishes to encourage others to try it. If, besides encouragement, the book is of assistance through the author's modest experience and enthusiastic study, then it will have been well worth the effort.

Members of the Kennolyn Riding School Vaulting Club, Soquel, California, posed for the photographs, which were taken by Antonin Vacek of Woodside, Mr. and Mrs. Norman Anthony of Salinas, and Mrs. June Fallaw of Pittsburg, all in California.

Line drawings are by Margaret Fuller of La Mesa, California.

E. F.

Foreword

In all the great arts, harmony plays a major part but in horsemanship it is essential. For years I have been searching for the key in teaching young riders harmony and rhythm with their horses. During my visit to California last year I was taken to a practice "vaulting" session at Kennolyn Summer Camp. I was fascinated. Here was my answer. The children, whilst learning to vault, were subconsciously picking up the beat, developing a sense of timing and co-ordination, and getting a feeling for the paces and movement of the horse. They had lost all sense of fear and thus were completely relaxed. Balance had become second nature and all the finer points of riding were falling into place.

That evening Mrs. Friedlaender showed me the early manuscript of this book. I thought it was excellent and spent the rest of my visit picking her brains. I learnt that she had been training successful vaulting teams for years and, being a perfectionist, had made an extensive study of the art of vaulting both in Germany and America.

During the last two summers I have had the pleasure of watching her instruct dressage. Not only is she an exceptional person and a brilliant rider, but she has all

FOREWORD

the qualities of a great teacher — patience, clear thinking, and that rare talent, an ability to impart her knowledge to others. This she has done throughout her book. In sharing the author's belief in vaulting, both as a sport and as an ideal grounding for competitive horsemanship, I am delighted to be associated with it.

I am hoping to start vaulting classes in England, when this book will be of immense value both to me and my pupils.

>The Lady Mary Rose Williams
>Willowbrook Cottage
>Turkdean
>Northleach, Gloucestershire

Introduction

Modern vaulting or gymnastics on the back of a cantering horse, as seen by the public today, is done mainly by children and is practiced most widely in Germany, where many riding schools have vaulting clubs for children. A national championship for vaulting teams is held in Germany each year.

It is also in modern times that most of the cavalries of the world, including our own, practiced vaulting as an integral part of the riding program. The Swiss dressage rider Gottfried Traschel (1952 and 1956 Olympics) was vaulting instructor at the Swiss Cavalry School in Thun. Other internationally famed riders for whom vaulting played a part in their beginnings, were the jump riders Helga Kohler and Fritz Thiedemann, both of Germany.

The 1920 Olympic Games, held in Antwerp, included for the first (and last) time in modern Olympics a competition in the form of a vaulting test on the standing, cantering, unsaddled, and saddled horse. Unfortunately, only three countries participated — Belgium and France, each with six competitors, and Sweden, with five. Germany, where vaulting was most popular, was in the throes of a political upheaval and did not take part in the 1920 Games. The competition was never repeated. However, we still have a form of riding gymnastics performed in the Games consisting of very formalized exercises on the leather horse; some of these exercises still have a resemblance to natural vaulting on the living horse.

Riding gymnastics go back to the Romans, and more

INTRODUCTION

recently to the era of German knighthood, when they were used as a preparation for riding itself. Then down through the centuries, riding gymnastics moved further and further away from natural exercises in preparation for riding, and became more and more stylized.

Therefore it is now with the youngsters that we once more discover the values and pleasures of gymnastics on the living horse. Whereas vaulting is done in Germany as a preparatory training for riding, in the United States in seems to be practiced in Pony clubs and other riding groups simultaneously with equitation, as a supplement and an aid.

In vaulting, the children become more supple and graceful in following the movement of the horse, their rhythm improves and they become more confident and courageous. In short, they truly become one with the horse — the goal of all serious riders.

Since writing the foregoing, the American Vaulting Association held its first championship competition, at Santa Cruz County Fair in Watsonville, California. Most of the teams registered with the AVA have been U.S. Pony club groups (including the all-boy team of the Palouse Hills Pony Club, Moscow, Idaho).

Also attesting the growth of vaulting in America was the first East Coast team to register with the Association — the Woodlane Vaulting Team of Mount Holly, New Jersey — and the fact that, after the first championship, thirteen candidates passed their AVA examinations for Senior and Junior vaulting judge.

Elizabeth Friedlaender
Molehaven
Soquel, California

Preparation

One of the most important elements of successful vaulting work is, of course, the horse. The countries having clubs devoted solely to vaulting enjoy the advantage of having beautifully trained horses that are kept and schooled for this purpose almost exclusively, and this is the ideal approach to the sport. However, when vaulting is only a part of the equitation program, such as it is in Pony clubs, it is most difficult to find someone on a purely volunteer basis who is willing to acquire, keep, and train a horse entirely for vaulting. It is feasible, though, to look among the children's mounts for one or more animals that will not object too much to this sort of periodic activity!

Ideally, vaulting is taught only on a cantering horse, since at the canter the rhythm of the gait is the easiest for the vaulter to follow. The energy of the gait gives the youngster the necessary assistance, through impulsion, for execution of the exercises. Nevertheless, since we are very often faced with training the horse and the young vaulters simultaneously, we may find it expedient to start out doing many of the exercises with the horse at a standstill, and to progress gradually through the walk, trot, and finally the canter. In this way the child and the horse build up confidence in the work and in each other.

PREPARATION

EQUIPMENT

Besides the horse — whose specifics will be discussed in a moment — the equipment needed for vaulting is:

1. *A vaulting surcingle:* it is equipped with two hand-grips; a loop for the foot on the off side — or both sides (the latter is best but must be ordered especially); a ring on top with a stand-up rein, and rings on the sides for fastening side reins.
2. A snaffle bridle
3. Longe line
4. Side reins
5. Longeing whip

The surcingle must be well fitted and padded over the withers — leather-lined is best. The grips must be well enough sprung away from the girth to allow the hands to slip in and out easily without rubbing knuckles. Rigid handles are of more help to the vaulter in attaining elevation over the horse than are flexible handles.

A felt pad under the surcingle is helpful to keep the youngsters from slipping during practice. (In competition a pad is not allowed, but rosin is often used.) A sheepskin protector to guard the horse from being chafed is highly recommended and can be ordered with the surcingle. Surcingles can be secured readily from the leading saddlemakers in Germany (*see* Appendix).

For ordinary practice work, a longeing cavesson may be used with side reins attached. When the horse is used to being longed on a snaffle bridle, the reins can be done up out of the way through the throatlash, or removed;

EQUIPMENT

the longe line run through the near side bit-ring, up over the head, and snapped to the off bit-ring (in the so-called French manner), and side reins attached. This manner of fixing the longe line keeps the weight of it from pulling the bit through the mouth. For competitions and exhibitions, the reins are removed from the bridle and only the side reins used. The longe line can also be run through the near side snaffle-ring, under the chin, and attached to the off side bit-ring, or to a ring on a strap connecting the two bit-rings.

Pipsqueak ready for practice, with snaffle bridle, side reins, leather-lined web surcingle, felt practice pad (not allowed in competition), sheepskin protector, and longe line attached in the French manner. The stand-up rein (for beginners) would be snapped to the surcingle between the grips.

PREPARATION

Side reins are necessary in order to keep the horse's neck straight and to keep the head position as steady as possible. They should be unsnapped at rest periods.

DRESS

The vaulters should be dressed in easy-fitting short-sleeved or sleeveless shirts, and shorts (in some groups the girls wear short skirts with matching undershorts). *Tennis shoes must be worn.* For any kind of a competition or exhibition, the dress should be uniform in style and color.

THE HORSE

An important requisite, before putting very much time on the training of a horse for this work, is that it have a well-balanced slow canter which it can maintain without effort or coercion. Many horses are suitable for work at the walk and trot, but it is not easy to find among the average Pony club horses such a mover at the canter.

A further requirement in selecting any horse to be used for this work is that it be very obedient on the longe line. There is absolutely no use trying anything with the animal until this training is established — moreover, it is dangerous.

The size of the horse is not too important. In working with small children exclusively, a small horse or pony is, of course, very nice. However, most vaulting groups are mixed, and it is amazing how quite small children are able to learn to vault onto horses 15.3 hands in height.

THE HORSE

Having horses of several sizes is, naturally, of great advantage — but this will also call for considerable differences in the size of the surcingle, which, due to the nature of its construction, is normally limited in how much it can be adjusted. However, the manufacturers have come up with an extension piece that makes it possible to use a smaller surcingle on a larger horse.

The vaulting horse shown in the photographs is Pipsqueak, an aged gray mare of unknown breeding, one out of a string of horses in a local riding school. She is 14.2 hands high, built like a miniature Percheron with a broad back for kneeling and standing, has a rather stylish way of going, with smooth gaits, and is very gentle *and* very smart. The team loves her passionately. They have complete confidence in her good nature, and have won their share of competitions as a result of their confidence. The vaulters working with her range from five to twenty-one years old.

To make a good horse for vaulting, the youngsters must be encouraged to make much of him right from the start: much petting and handling, crawling all over him, and rewarding him with tidbits. It will soon be apparent whether or not the animal is going to object; and naturally, if there are any tendencies toward kicking when being touched around the hind legs or persistent bucking when the weight of a vaulter comes too far back, the horse must be rejected. Many times the adverse reaction to weight far back is due to a physical weakness or problem in that region, and it would therefore be abusing the animal to persist in attempting to use him for vaulting work.

Even beginning vaulters can help train the horse by getting him used to them at a standstill, while the more

PREPARATION

experienced ones can begin the training at a trot and then move up to a canter.

One of the most difficult things to overcome is the horse's tendency to slow down or stop whenever anyone runs toward him along the longe line, or when anyone jumps off his back. This difficulty is overcome by having the experienced vaulters get on at a standstill. Then the instructor starts the horse moving and has them vault off and run alongside the horse, while the instructor concentrates on keeping the animal moving. When the youngsters can vault off at all gaits and run alongside, and the horse will keep his gait, we are ready to start "running at him" to vault on.

A note of caution here: Never allow the mounted vaulters to hit or kick the horse to keep him going. Beginning vaulters are very awkward and do quite a bit of accidental kicking and banging. If the horse is going to interpret such thumps as a signal to increase the gait, disaster is sure to come sooner or later.

In order to avoid having to become rough and thereby frightening the horse while teaching him to allow the children to approach him rapidly, it is best to follow the routine of beginning first at the walk, then the trot, and finally the canter.

With the horse at the walk, the vaulter stands at the instructor's side and then moves out along the longe at the walk, in step with the horse, to the horse's shoulder. With hands on the grips of the surcingle, he walks along, keeping his shoulders parallel with those of the horse.

When the horse will accept this and keep walking along, he is then put at a trot, and the youngster repeats

WARM-UP

the procedure, always in step with the horse, trotting at the shoulder, holding the grips.

And finally, we are ready to repeat the lesson at a canter, the child cantering on the same lead as the horse. Depending upon the horse (and of course how often he is worked), this may take a couple of days or a week — or perhaps longer in some cases. Only quiet patience will produce the desired results.

Since most children are right-handed, vaulting is more easily done with the horse going to the left. It is occasionally beneficial, though, for the youngsters to work awhile going to the right. And it is very important for the horse that he either be used part of the period on the right hand or that he be longed during his warm-up on the right, so that he does not become too one-sided.

Whereas a horse can be used as much as an hour at the standstill, walk, and trot, the limit should be about 40 minutes when working mainly at the canter, and this includes rests between exercises. It is just as important to keep the horse from becoming mentally tired and irritated as it is to watch over his physical well-being.

WARM-UP

The importance of warm-up exercises on the ground prior to vaulting must not be overlooked. The vaulters are thus afforded an opportunity to loosen up their muscles and develop some spring, so they don't waste the valuable energy of the horse merely to limber themselves. Some vaulting clubs devote much time to "ground" gymnastics, including work on the leather horse, tumbling, and acrobatics such as handstands,

Leapfrogging to develop spring and form — but the boy's legs should be stretched more, and his toes pointed down.

cartwheels, etc. Tumbling can be particularly valuable, in that the youngster learns how to break a fall by doubling up and rolling or somersaulting. If a group has the time and facilities, there can be no doubt as to the over-all value of such activities.

Even for groups that vault on a more casual and informal basis, however, there is still a minimum of ground warm-up which should not be neglected. Such

Next is practice in the Vault-on over the Croup, and here the boy's form is good: excellent spring and elevation, with arms already rising to be well stretched out when he lands.

PREPARATION

exercises include jumping sideways over a rope (or longe line) whose ends are held by two people at a height of 12 to 18 inches off the ground. Facing either end of the rope, the youngster jumps back and forth over it several times, pulling up his knees very high while keeping his toes pointed downward, and springing as high off the ground as possible.

Next, leapfrog should be practiced in a long line, the children taking turns going down the entire line from the rear. They bend over just far enough to put their hands on their knees (heads down!), so as to make a good height for the jump. They should take care to jump from both feet with legs stretched straight and toes pointed.

Leapfrogging should be immediately followed by using the same leap to jump over the croup of the standing horse into the Riding Seat.

HOW TO BEGIN THE WORK

There are no hard and fast rules concerning how one should begin the vaulting instruction, but a number of factors must be taken into consideration: the age of the children, the training of the horse, and whether you have an experienced vaulter to demonstrate. When one is working with youngsters over twelve years of age, if the horse will allow them to run at it, at least at a trot, and if one has an experienced vaulter to demonstrate, the following method works very well.

At the beginning of each session the instructor establishes an order of going, which the vaulters adhere to throughout the lesson. Not only does this save the in-

Correct form for the simple Vault-on: in step with the horse, head up, ready for her spring forward on both feet.

structor's time and voice, but also the horse's energy. Equally important, the attention of the children is maintained — it requires them to be alert and watchful at all times so as not to miss their turns. While one youngster is working, the next one must stand at the instructor's side, ready to take over as the first vaulter finishes. When the horse is moving, the instructor raises the longeing whip for the next child to pass under for his turn.

The children will first be taught how to run to the horse properly and take hold of the hand-grips. The demonstrator trots out toward the horse, staying always

HOW TO BEGIN THE WORK

right alongside the longe line *but never taking hold of it*. From the moment he starts, he picks up the rhythm of the horse in his own step and also the correct footing: that is, his left foot is moving with the left forefoot of the horse, his right foot with the horse's right fore. When he has come into position to vault on, he is in perfect rhythm and step and does not have to waste time trying to find the correct stride and footing.

As soon as the demonstrator reaches the horse, he trots next to him at the shoulder, facing forward, and takes the hand-grips with both hands. He trots alongside in this manner, keeping his shoulders always parallel with those of the horse and his whole body as close to the horse as possible — he must not have his shoulders next to the horse and his hips and feet a foot or more away! Nor may he face the horse at any time. His head is up, eyes looking forward, not down.

The demonstrator trots along until the instructor gives the signal to break away, whereupon he drops away from the horse several steps toward the inside of the circle. After the horse has safely passed, he can leave the circle to the outside, away from the instructor. A vaulter must not simply let go and allow the horse to trot closely by, as he could very easily be kicked. Each youngster in turn then repeats this exercise until all can move easily out into vaulting position and trot with the horse correctly and confidently.

Next, the experienced vaulter mounts the horse and demonstrates the correct vault into the Riding Seat, or "vault-on," and the basic Vault-off to the Inside (for descriptions and diagrams of these two exercises, see "The Six Compulsory Vaulting Exercises" and "Dismounts," respectively, in the next chapter). Each youngster in turn

PREPARATION

is given a leg-up at the standstill to practice correct form for these two exercises. They are then practiced at a walk and trot. After watching the demonstrator several times, the children may now make their first attempts to vault on at a trot. It should be understood that many may not succeed during the first few lessons, but they should be encouraged to keep trying, for they will get it sooner or later.

For a class of eight to twelve youngsters, the work described above would occupy one practice period. If progress warrants it, all this could be repeated at a canter at the next practice period. However, if the horse as yet requires too much stimulation or coercion from the instructor to maintain the canter, it is better to perfect the exercises at a trot and wait until the canter is steady.

Scissors Kick

After the Riding Seat and simple Vault-off to the Inside have been learned, we generally start practicing the "scissors kick" shown in Figure 1, since most exercises involve high swinging or kicking with the legs.

Holding on to the grips, the vaulter swings both legs forward, then back and upward as high over the horse's back as possible. The legs are kept absolutely straight *with toes pointed* from the beginning of the forward swing. At the apex of the backward swing, the legs and feet must be together. The swing must be made with freedom, not by dragging the legs stiffly along the horse's sides. In order to get backward height with the legs, the vaulter's head and shoulders drop low along the inside of the horse's neck, but the line of the vaulter's

HOW TO BEGIN THE WORK

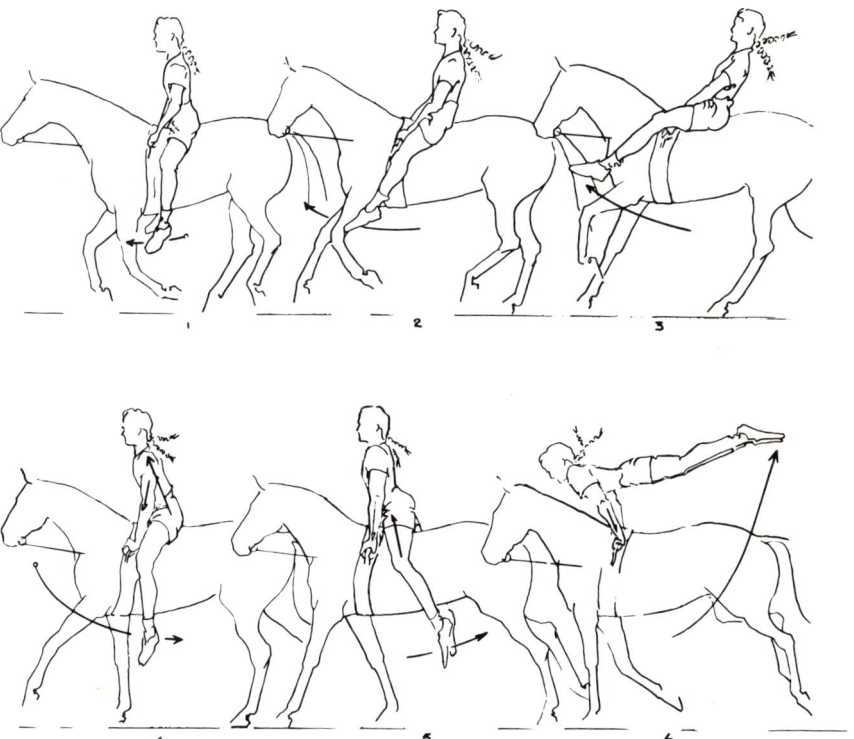

Figure 1. Scissors Kick

back must remain straight. Keeping the weight of balance over the wrists and pushing strongly with the arms will bring about the maximum elevation of the entire body over the horse's back.

We cannot stress pointed toes too much! Particularly in this exercise, the effect of the toes is most apparent: when not pointed, the swing will drag and the knees will bend; when pointed, everything goes with ease. The kick must be made with one graceful, sweeping swing — not start with bent knees and end with a frog kick to

PREPARATION

straighten the legs. In trying to master this "scissors kick," some young beginners become so tense and tired that it is best to discontinue practicing it for a while and go on to another exercise that they are able to do better, thus giving them a feeling of accomplishment rather than failure.

It is also helpful, when a vaulter is having trouble with an exercise, to have him dismount and watch someone who can do it with ease. Just seeing someone do the exercise freely, very often makes all the difference in his own approach. With patience and encouragement, all children will learn to swing the legs and attain proper elevation over the back of the horse, no matter how hopeless it may look in the first few attempts.

Even though the leg-swings may leave much to be desired, after a number of attempts we let the vaulter go on to complete the compulsory Scissors, by crossing one leg over the other at the apex of the backswing, rolling the body with the crossing leg, and returning to a sitting position facing the rear end of the horse. (The Scissors, required for competition, is described more fully and diagramed in Figure 2 in the next chapter.)

As a matter of course we always have an experienced vaulter demonstrate an exercise many times, doing it as slowly as possible. However, if an experienced vaulter is not available or if we are working with a particularly timid youngster, we may have to resort to other means — break the exercise into parts, or "drag" through it. For instance, in order to let the vaulter get the feel of the scissors kick — the position of the legs and the turn of the body — we drag through the exercise on the standing horse, as follows.

Holding on to the grips, the youngster lies on his

HOW TO BEGIN THE WORK

stomach with legs stretched out full length along the horse's back. He then puts his left leg over his right and turns his body to the left, facing the horse's near side. As soon as he feels the mechanics of the turn, he is ready to practice it with the necessary high leg-swing.

* * *

From this point on, new exercises and experiences can be added at the discretion of the instructor, keeping in mind that previous work must be constantly perfected in form, and enough new work added to keep the class eager. Such things as the Stand and the Cossack Hang (both later, in "The Six Compulsory Exercises" and "Single Kür Exercises," respectively) can be introduced at a standstill and a walk very early in the instruction in order to give the youngsters confidence in unusual positions.

We cannot be dogmatic about the sequence to be followed, for there is too much difference in the children's physical build and strength, suppleness, co-ordination, and mental approach (timidity or fear). If some of the vaulters have had no previous riding experience, considerable time will have to be spent letting them just sit on the moving horse, first holding onto the grips; then later they can practice going with arms outstretched, hands on hips, swinging and rotating the arms, twisting the trunk, etc., until they can sit supplely and confidently and move easily with the horse at all gaits.

If the group is more or less uniform in ability and experience, it is a good idea to work on one particular thing at a time with the entire group, each youngster taking his turn to try the exercise once. Using this method,

PREPARATION

full attention is maintained, the youngsters watch each other with more interest, and do not have to wait endlessly for their turns. A group of eight to twelve children is the ideal number for a class. If the group is larger, the individual must wait too long for his turn; if smaller, each youngster will tire more quickly.

The Riding Seat, first of the Compulsory Exercises, with the vaulter's body well aligned with the horse.

Building the Foundation

THE SIX COMPULSORY EXERCISES

In vaulting competitions there are two types of exercises: the *Pflicht* (required or compulsory exercises) and the *Kür* (artistic, free-style presentation of other exercises and combinations). The six Compulsory Exercises are the basic groundwork of all vaulting, just as the practicing of scales is to a pianist. The order in which they are described follows the order in which they are performed in a competition, but may not necessarily be the order in which they are taught.

Vaulting exercises are "begun" and "finished." The beginning is the vault-on into the Riding Seat. The finish is the dismount, and varies with the exercise.

EXERCISE	DISMOUNT
1. Vault into Riding Seat	Vault-off to Inside
2. Kneel* and Flag	Vault-off to Inside
3. The Mill	Vault-off to Inside
4. The Flank	Vault-off to Outside
5. The Stand	Half-flank to Inside
6. Scissors	Half-flank to Inside

* After this was written, the German rules dispensed with the free Kneel as a formal component of the second Compulsory Exercise.

BUILDING THE FOUNDATION

1. Vault into Riding Seat

Ideally, the vault into the Riding Seat should be taught right from the start on a cantering horse. This is because the effort of the vault-on is made much easier for the youngster by the impulsion and rhythm of the gait, and there will be a much smaller chance of getting into wrong form. The child is first taught to run on the left lead with the horse. From the moment he leaves the instructor's side until he actually vaults on, this lead and the rhythm of the canter must be maintained.

The youngster runs out to the horse along the longe line. As soon as he catches hold of the grips, he faces forward and canters in step alongside, shoulders parallel to those of the horse, eyes up and looking forward. Then with an energetic spring forward on both feet, as in Figure 2, he raises the right leg high over the horse's back, left leg stretched down straight with toe pointed, and comes smoothly into the Riding Seat immediately behind the surcingle. The vaulter then stretches his arms out, shoulder high or slightly higher, palms down, fingers together, thumbs under, and sits straight and supplely, legs hanging stretched with toes pointed. *This position is held for at least four strides.*

It is essential that while on the ground cantering at the horse's side, the youngster be right at the surcingle or slightly in advance of it, so that the spring forward will take him as far forward as possible. This will ensure maximum impulsion from his spring as the horse passes him.

If the youngster allows himself to be dragged along behind the surcingle, he will get no assistance from the horse, and his spring will take him too far back on the horse. Not staying far enough forward, not jumping far

THE SIX COMPULSORY EXERCISES

Figure 2.   Vault into Riding Seat (simple Vault-on)

enough forward, leading with the knee of the right leg instead of the toe, and not jumping off of both feet are very common faults and are responsible for most of the mounting difficulties. *For competitive purposes, the vault-on must be begun within four strides after taking hold of the grips.*

If work is being done at the trot, the same principles apply. The youngsters must move in rhythm and footing with the horse at all times.

BUILDING THE FOUNDATION

2. The Flag

From the Riding Seat, the vaulter swings his legs forward and pushes strongly with his arms to lift his knees smoothly into place behind the surcingle. (A much harder and more flashy method is to start with a forward swing of the legs for impulsion. As the legs swing back and up, the knees are tucked under, the legs come together and the vaulter comes to rest on his knees, immediately behind the surcingle. This must be done softly so as not to abuse the horse's back.) In the kneeling posi-

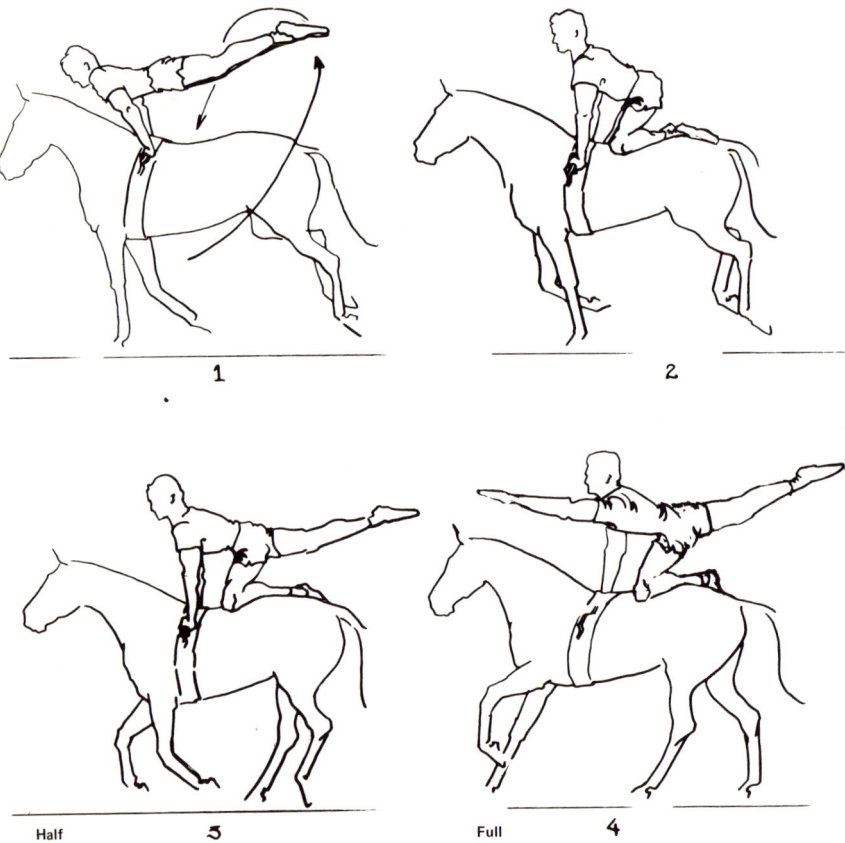

Figure 3. The Flag

THE SIX COMPULSORY EXERCISES

tion the toes lie flat, following the curve of the horse's back, and must not dig in.

To complete the free Kneel, the vaulter then lets go of the grips, straightens up on his knees with back straight, head up, eyes forward, and streches his arms out horizontally, even with his shoulders, fingers together, palms down, thumbs tucked under. *This position is held for at least four strides.*

Note: The free Kneel is no longer required as part of the second Compulsory Exercise, viz. footnote earlier.

The grips are then retaken to develop the Flag, so named because the extended right leg waves up and down like a banner with the movement of the horse.

To perform the Flag from the kneeling position, the vaulter first puts his left leg and foot across the horse's back so that the left toe is on the right side of the horse. This position of the left leg, which can be seen in the photograph, keeps the left knee from slipping off the horse. The right leg is then extended to the rear at a level slightly higher than the vaulter's back, which must be flat and straight. The right leg must be perfectly straight with toe pointed, the head must be up and the eyes forward. At this point, with both hands still holding the grips, the vaulter has performed the Half-Flag. This much of the exercise is practiced for a time, until the correct form has been mastered.

To complete the Flag the vaulter next extends his left arm straight forward from the shoulder, palm down, fingers closed, thumb under. The fingertips of the left hand and the toe of the right foot should be on a level. Head up! Eyes forward!

BUILDING THE FOUNDATION

This is a very pretty exercise when done properly and, like many of the others, is not nearly as easy at it looks! The vaulter must remember to keep the weight well forward over his right arm so that his back will remain straight. Otherwise everything from the hips backward will droop most unattractively.

The Flag, second Compulsory Exercise. It would be more harmonious if she turned her hand up more from the wrist, to make the arm and leg lines better balanced.

Stressing form: The only flaw in the Riding Seat, above, is the slight sweep-back of the right arm; but the free Kneel, below (no longer required in the Flag), has good stretch.

BUILDING THE FOUNDATION

3. The Mill

In the Mill the vaulter is required to make a complete turn on the back of the horse. (Figure 4.)

Starting from the Riding Seat, the first phase is the side-seat position to the inside, accomplished by carrying the right leg as high as possible across the neck of the horse. The second phase brings the rider to the Riding Seat facing the croup, by carrying the left leg high across the croup. The third phase is the side-seat position to the outside — that is, the right, or off side — by swinging the right leg as high as possible across the croup. The fourth and final phase finds the vaulter once more in the riding seat facing forward, having lifted the left leg high over the neck of the horse (Step 8).

The whole essence of this exercise is that it be done in perfect rhythm and form. The vaulter must count the strides and move his legs on the same count each time.

In competition, the movements may be made on every second, third or fourth stride, but *whichever rhythm is selected, must be maintained throughout the exercise.* Most competitive vaulters use every fourth stride.

Each leg must be carried straight, as high as possible, with pointed toes. The upper body leans back to allow maximum elevation of the legs from the hips. The hands change on the grips as needed, and as rapidly as possible in order to keep the seat secure. To do this exercise correctly takes considerable practice — in fact, although simple in pattern and rather unspectacular to watch, it is one of the hardest to do in good form.

The exercise is finished with a Vault-off to the Inside, in the same rhythm as the rest of the exercise — i.e., a two-, three- or four-count rhythm.

THE SIX COMPULSORY EXERCISES

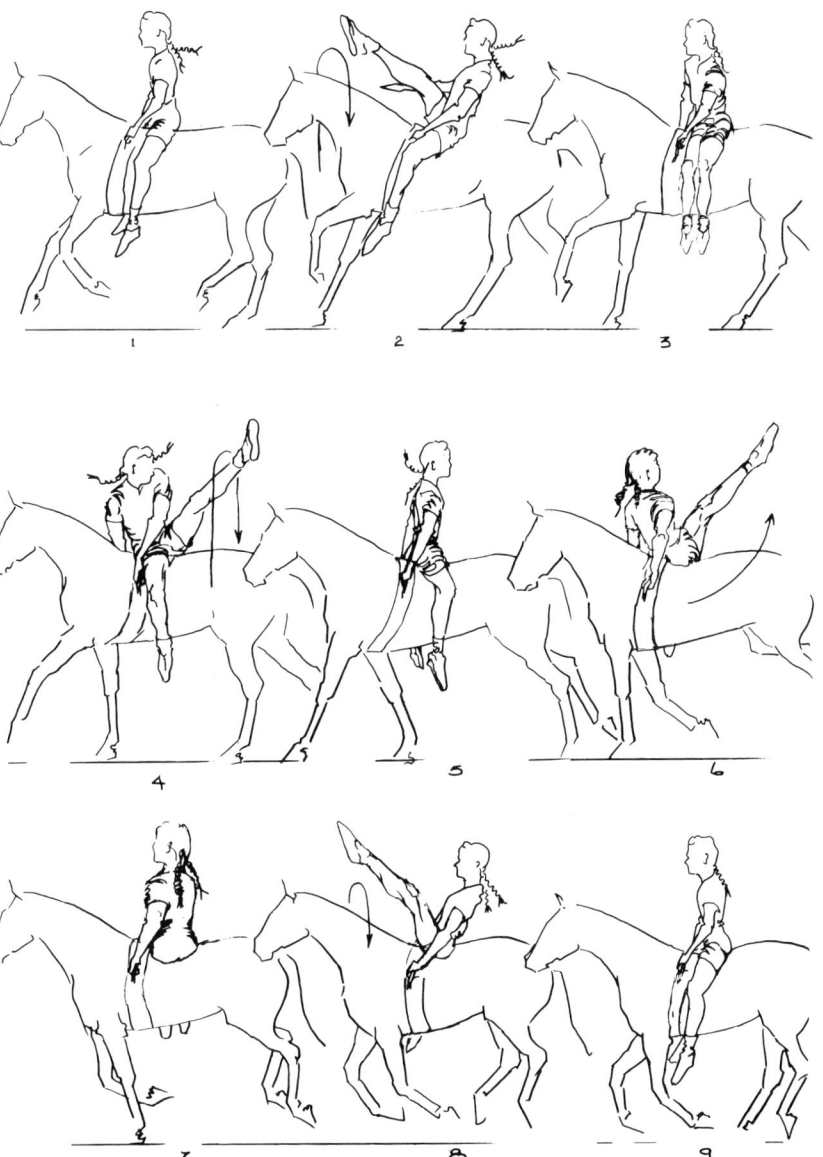

Figure 4. The Mill

BUILDING THE FOUNDATION

4. The Flank

The Flank (diagramed in Figure 5) is begun from the vault into the Riding Seat.

The upper body leans back as the legs are swung energetically forward in order to develop impulsion for swinging the legs very high behind (as in Steps 1 and 2). At the height of the swing, with the legs together, the hips are tucked and the legs "jackknifed" forward, bringing the vaulter into the side-seat position to the inside, squarely on his seat (Steps 3 and 4). It he does not tuck at the hips, he will come onto his stomach or his right hip, and will have to readjust his position before continuing.

Within four canter strides, the legs are again energetically swung together high over the horse's back; the body is supported by the arms, which are straight and firm with no bend at the elbows. The vaulter's center of gravity is over the grips (approximately his waistline, as in Step 5), the arms slanting back from the shoulders, legs straight and together, toes pointed. Again at the height of the swing, the hips are tucked, legs curving forward, and at the same time the vaulter pushes back strongly with his arms so that he arcs through the air and lands with legs together, close to the horse. From side-seat position on the left side, to the ground on the right side, is all one fluid movement.

The vaulter immediately picks up the canter rhythm *on the left lead for two strides,* and then moves away from the horse.

THE SIX COMPULSORY EXERCISES

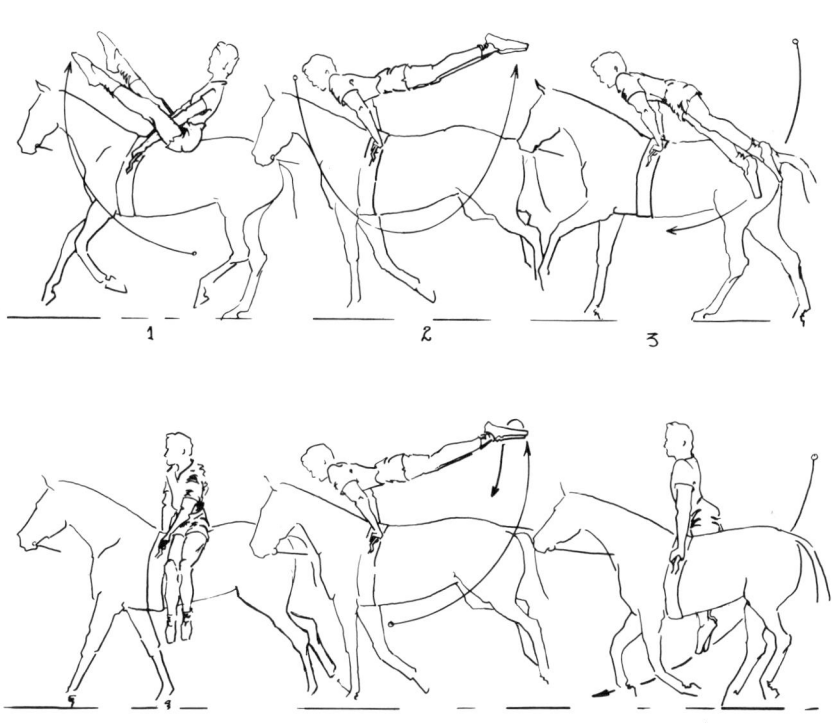

Figure 5. The Flank

BUILDING THE FOUNDATION

5. The Stand

The Stand is developed from the kneeling position. The vaulter first jumps from the Riding Seat to his knees, following immediately with a jump to his feet in a squatting position (onto both feet simultaneously, *not* one foot at a time). Both feet are close to the surcingle, with the left foot slightly in advance of the right. He takes the stand-up rein in his right hand. As he straightens up, he first lets go of the right grip. As he then lets go of the left grip, he takes the stand-up rein in both hands, keeping his knees slightly bent. As confidence grows, the youngster can let go of the stand-up rein with the left hand, holding that arm out to the side. And then, finally, he can let go of the rein entirely, and put both arms out to the side in the free Stand.

When the youngsters reach open competition level, they do not use the stand-up rein at all — in fact it is usually removed from the surcingle, as it often gets in the way under the seat or legs of the vaulters.

To return to the Riding Seat, the vaulter leans over and takes the grips, and then drops softly down into the Riding Seat, taking the weight on his arms so that there is no blow to the horse's back.

This exercise is finished with a Half-Flank to the Inside (see "Dismounts," later).

THE SIX COMPULSORY EXERCISES

A good free Stand, with vaulter erect and knees slightly flexed to follow the horse's action.

BUILDING THE FOUNDATION

6. Scissors

The Scissors is performed from the Riding Seat.

As indicated in Figure 6, the vaulter's legs are swung energetically forward, then as high as possible to the rear, legs stretched straight, toes pointed; and while in the air (as near the height of the swing as possible), the body turns to the left, the left (or inner) leg crosses over the right to the right side of the horse. The hands are changed on the grips as the vaulter seats himself facing the rear of the horse.

The longer the youngster holds the *original* grip position, the more sure he will be to come into centered riding seat position facing the rear, directly behind the surcingle. The more slowly this exercise is performed, the more beautiful it is, as the vaulter has much more control of the swing and elevation of the body.

THE SIX COMPULSORY EXERCISES

Figure 6.   Scissors

BUILDING THE FOUNDATION

The return Scissors:

To return to the Riding Seat facing forward (Figure 7), the vaulter first leans forward in order to swing the legs back for an energetic swing forward (Step 1). Then, as the legs swing forward, the torso leans far back in order to free the hips and allow the legs to come as high as possible. (As the vaulter becomes stronger and more supple, he will be able to raise his hips completely off the horse by pushing strongly with his arms, and by the energy of his upward swing — as in Step 3. When his hips can be lifted thus, the return Scissors becomes truly spectacular.) At the height of the swing forward, the right leg crosses over the left (Step 4). The hands are changed on the grips as the vaulter comes into the Riding Seat facing forward again.

A Half-Flank to the Inside finishes the exercise.

THE SIX COMPULSORY EXERCISES

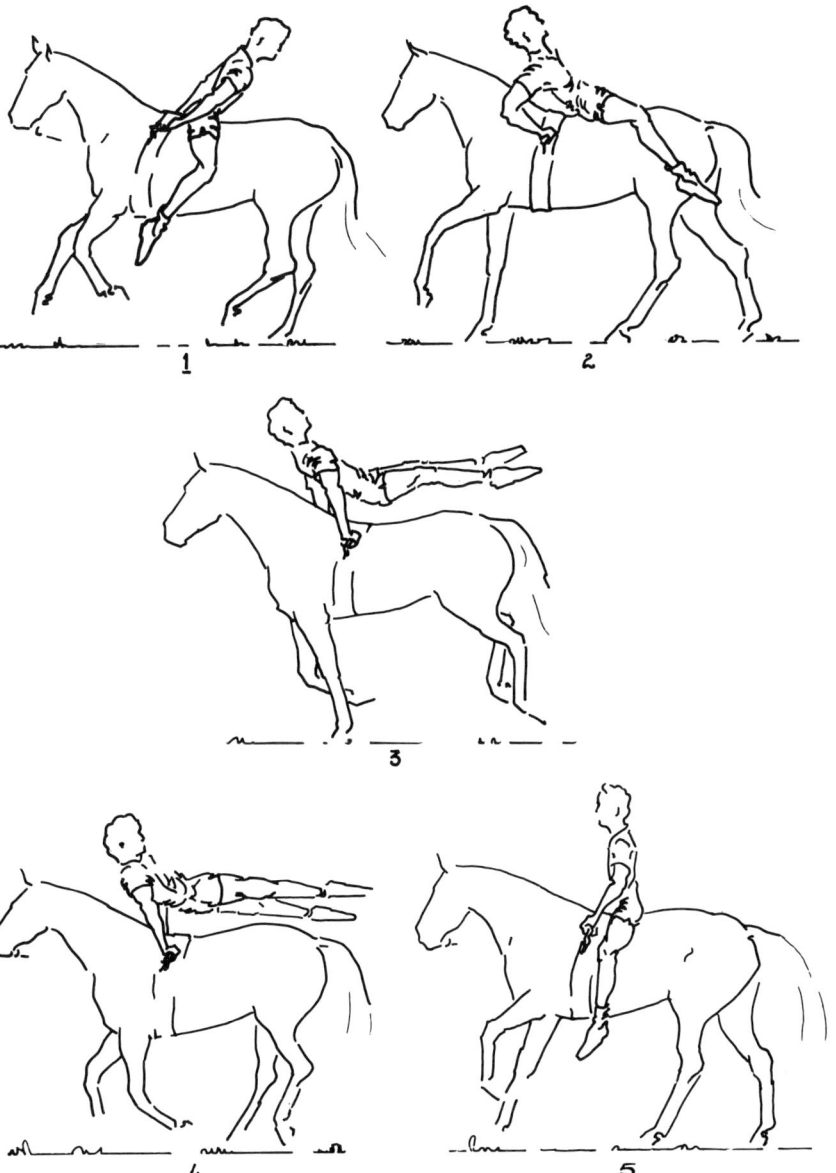

Figure 7. Return Scissors

BUILDING THE FOUNDATION

DISMOUNTS FOR COMPULSORY EXERCISES

Vault-off to the Inside

To execute the Vault-off to the Inside, which is the basic vault-off for most exercises, the youngster is in the Riding Seat holding the grips with both hands. He swings his right leg up as high as possible and across the neck of the horse (leg straight, toe pointed!), letting go of the grips in turn to let the leg pass, then retaking the grips. When the right leg is in place beside the left (not specified in Figure 8, but putting the vaulter in a side seat with shoulders parallel to those of the horse, eyes forward). The vaulter dismounts by swinging the legs forward, absolutely together, landing with feet close to the horse, facing forward with hands still on the grips (unless the vaulter is too small to retain both grips). If the horse is moving, the youngster picks up the rhythm of the horse, *follows it for at least two strides* and then lets go and leaves the circle.

The whole execution, properly done, is one flowing movement with no pauses, particularly at the point where the right leg is brought across to the left side. However, it takes considerable practice to acquire the correct timing and rhythm so that the effect is neither rushed and blurred, nor slow and sticky.

DISMOUNTS FOR COMPULSORY EXERCISES

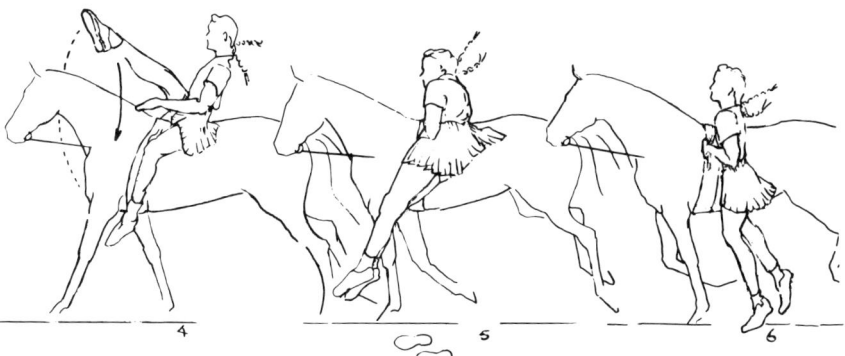

Figure 8. Simple Vault-off to the Inside

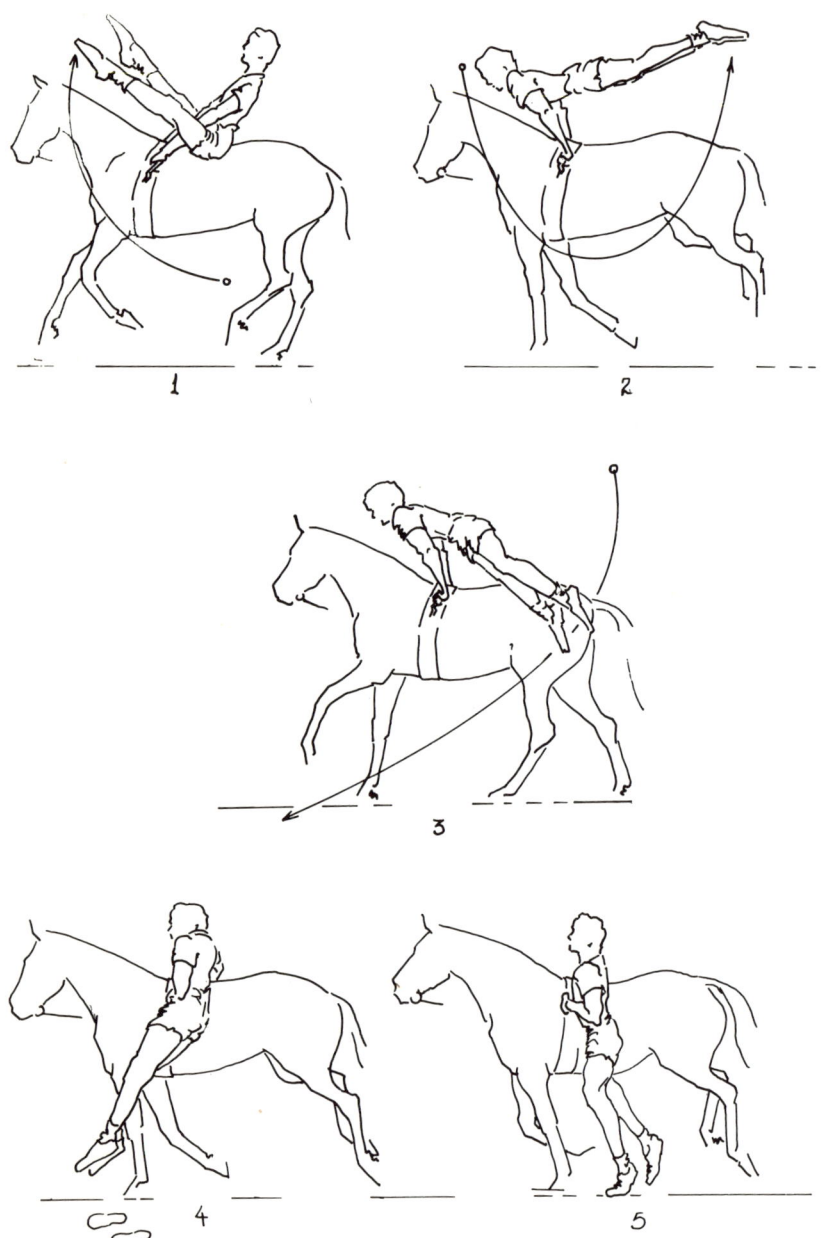

Figure 9. Half-Flank to the Inside

DISMOUNTS FOR COMPULSORY EXERCISES

Half-Flank to the Inside

The method of vaulting off called Half-Flank to the Inside is similar to the first part of an ordinary Flank — legs swung far forward to create impulsion for a high backswing with legs together, stretched straight, toes pointed (as in Step 2). The vaulter pushes strongly with arms and shoulders to gain as much body elevation as possible. Then instead of coming into the side seat on the inside (left), the vaulter lands on the ground on the inside, facing forward, shoulders parallel to those of the horse, feet close to the horse. It is essential that the legs remain together from the apex of the backswing until the vaulter touches the ground.

He then *canters two strides with the horse* before moving away.

Vault-off to the Outside

In a Vault-off to the Outside the vaulter comes down on the right side of the horse, facing forward, his feet close to the horse. He canters *on the left lead for two strides* before moving away from the horse.

This dismount is part of a continuous motion at the end of such an exercise as the Flank, for which it is the compulsory finish, and is in effect a Half-Flank to the Outside.

BUILDING THE FOUNDATION

Free Vault-off

The Free Vault-off to the Inside without use of the grips may or may not be demanded in the compulsory exercises. If well done, however, it is graded higher than the ordinary vault-off.

First, both hands let go of the grips. The right leg swings as high as possible over the horse's neck. At the same time the vaulter *must keep his left shoulder forward* by stretching his left arm forward, thus keeping himself from coming into a side-seat position. As the right leg comes over to join the left, the vaulter's arms move to keep the shoulders parallel with the shoulders of the horse, and he also strives to keep his hips as parallel with his shoulders as possible. When the right leg is on the descent, the left leg comes up to close with it, and the vaulter dismounts with both legs stretched forward and down. As he touches the ground, he brings both arms up horizontally as a graceful finish. The more slowly this exercise is performed, the easier it is for the vaulter to straighten his hips as he descends, so that he will be facing truly forward.

Caution: It is most important that the left shoulder counteract the swing of the right leg to prevent the side-seat position, for if the vaulter jumps to the ground from such a faulty position, he will not be facing forward — which will not only be awkward, *but could cause a fall.*

PRACTICE EXERCISES

Following are a few other individual exercises practiced simply to help the youngsters acquire suppleness and good form, and to add variety to the work.

PRACTICE EXERCISES

Side Seat to Astride

By passing the right leg across the neck of the horse, the vaulter comes from the Riding Seat into the side-seat position to the inside. As always, particular attention is paid to the height and straightness of the leg. In the side-seat position, it is important to keep the shoulders parallel to those of the horse. Then, leaning forward and taking the weight on the arms, pushing strongly for body elevation, the vaulter swings both legs back together, as high as possible over the back of the horse (toes pointed, legs straight!), and drops them down, one on each side of the horse, thereby returning to the riding seat. The Side Seat to Astride is practiced from both directions.

Side-to-Side

For the Side-to-Side, the vaulter starts out as if for Side Seat to Astride — first placing himself in the side-seat position to the inside and then passing the legs high together over the horse's back — *but now both legs come down together on the outside* (right), so that he is sitting in the side-seat position to the right.

This Side-to-Side is practiced several times in succession, passing from one side-seat position to the other.

In preparation for advanced work, this exercise can also be practiced by rotating the legs over the neck of the horse, as follows. After going from the side-seat position to the inside to the side seat outside, as described above, the vaulter then swings both legs high and straight over the horse's neck from the right side to the left side, and repeats the whole exercise several times, thereby describing a complete circle with his legs.

BUILDING THE FOUNDATION

Three-quarter Scissors from Side Seat

The Three-quarter Scissors from the side-seat position on the inside calls for a 270° roll of the body to the *right* to complete the turn (and is *not* just making a 90° turn of the body to the left by putting the right leg over the back of the horse).

Figure 10 indicates how the vaulter, sitting straight with his shoulders parallel to those of the horse, drops his weight forward to give his legs complete freedom of movement, turns his body to the right, at the same time swinging both legs up behind and passing his left leg under his right, finishing in the Riding Seat facing backward.

When done well, this exercise can be used as a single *Kür* exercise, finished by a Vault-off over the Croup or by a Flip-off — swinging the left leg high over the horse's neck, turning the body toward the left, and coming to the ground on the inside, facing forward.

PRACTICE EXERCISES

Figure 10. Three-quarter Scissors

BUILDING THE FOUNDATION

Downs-and-Ups

From the Riding Seat, the right leg is brought over the horse's neck as for a simple vault-off. Next, by counting and catching the rhythm of the horse, the youngster slides down with legs absolutely together, straight, toes pointed, shoulders parallel to those of the horse, eyes forward, *legs stretched far forward,* then hits the ground with both feet with enough impulsion and spring to jump immediately back onto the horse into the Riding Seat — or the side-seat position to the inside or outside, or Scissors-on — with no intervening stride.

The exercise can also be practiced from a Half-Flank to the Inside, as for the vault-off from Scissors or the Stand. However, this requires a little more skill in timing. In the simple vault-off, one can slow the descent somewhat by means of friction against the shoulder of the horse, if one's timing is a little off. But once committed to the air in the Half-Flank, there is very little adjustment that can be made if the timing is off.

Various combinations of these Downs-and-Ups are often used in the Kür and in exhibitions.

Leg Pass

To perform the Leg Pass, starting from the Riding Seat:

The right leg is brought over the neck of the horse and, in a continuous movement, passes under the left leg and on over the back of the horse to its original position in the Riding Seat. This would constitute one revolution of the Leg Pass. In practice, several consecutive revolutions are made so that there is one continuous motion in perfect rhythm with no obvious start or stop.

Advanced Work for Vaulting Teams

MOUNTING VARIATIONS

For exhibition purposes and for competition *Kür*, there are several additional ways of mounting which are very effective: the Vault into the Side Seat to the inside, or to the outside, directly to the knees, and the Scissors-on. Some very athletic boys are even able to vault on from the outside side-rear over the croup of the cantering horse!

Vault into Side Seat to the Inside

In making this jump, the vaulter must spring off very energetically and at the same time push very strongly with the arms. There is no help from the upswinging right leg, as for the vault into the Riding Seat. The legs remain as nearly together as possible, and it is a matter of thrusting strongly enough with the legs and arms to bring the seat of the vaulter to the back of the horse.

When well done, this is a graceful-looking exercise.

ADVANCED WORK

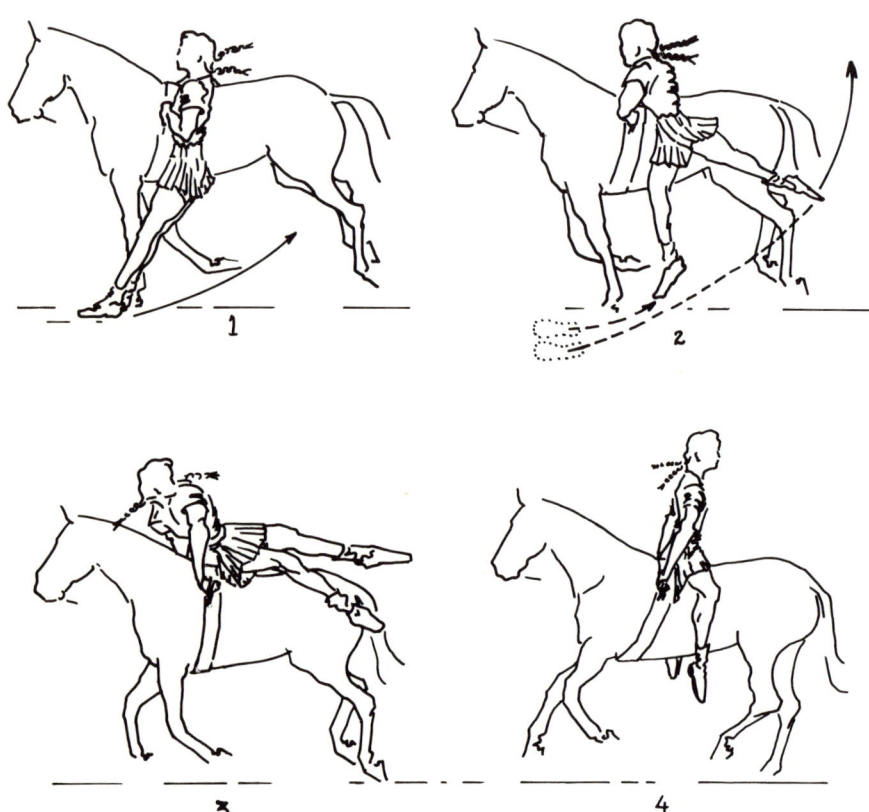

Figure 11. Scissors Vault-on

MOUNTING VARIATIONS

Scissors Vault-on

The Scissors Vault-on is a difficult exercise to do well, but when performed correctly is quite spectacular. It is another exercise that requires a particularly energetic spring forward by the vaulter. The left leg, instead of the right, is swung back and as high as possible over the croup to the right side of the horse, the vaulter's hips turning as the leg swings, bringing him into the Riding Seat facing the tail (Figure 11). If the swing is not high and energetic enough, the vaulter will come into a side-seat position to the inside.

A very nice finish for this exercise is a Vault-off over the Croup.

A rather spectacular alternative vault-off is for the vaulter to place his hands on the croup, swing the left leg high and back over the horse's neck, and at the same time push off with the hands and turn the body to the *left,* to land on both feet on the inside next to the croup, facing forward. This vault-off is called a Flip-off.

Vault into Side Seat to the Outside

This method of vaulting on is identical with the Free Flank (described in a moment), except that instead of dropping to the ground on the right side of the horse, the vaulter comes to rest in a side-seat position to the outside.

ADVANCED WORK

SINGLE KÜR EXERCISES

Following are some of the most frequently used individual exercises in the *Kür* portion of competition, as well as in exhibitions.

Cossack Hang

For the Cossack Hang there is a special loop provided on the off side of the surcingle, or on both sides when specially requested. The vaulter first puts his right foot into the loop over the ankle so that it will not slip off. Next, he puts himself in the side-seat position to the outside by bringing his left leg over the neck of the horse. He then lowers his body until he is hanging upside down on the left side of the horse with his left leg pointing vertically skyward with pointed toe, arms hanging straight down over his head toward the ground. *He remains in this position for four strides.*

To return to a sitting position, he gives a vigorous downward swing with the left leg, using the momentum to right his body until he can catch hold of the handgrips again.

If the youngster is very timid about letting his body hang down, he can at first use the standing rein as long as he can reach the end of it, so he feels more secure about the position.

Most youngsters like to do this exercise but it should not be compulsory in their training. They should be allowed to come to it in their own time when they feel ready — or not at all, if they do not wish to. It is first

SINGLE KÜR EXERCISES

In this Cossack Hang the vaulter's left leg is well forward, arms are even and well stretched.

ADVANCED WORK

A very well-done Shoulder Stand, with good balance, good stretch, feet together and toes pointed.

SINGLE KÜR EXERCISES

practiced at a standstill and often it is better to let the children proceed through walk and trot before trying it at a canter.

Shoulder Stand

The Shoulder Stand is developed from the kneeling position. The vaulter's right shoulder is placed in the groove of the withers so that his head is on the left side of the horse. He then pushes off to balance on his shoulder, supported by his hands on the grips. The legs must be straight and together with toes pointed, back arched and vertical. Some vaulters find it easier to take both legs up nearly simultaneously — others raise first the right, then the left. Some particularly strong vaulters can come into the Shoulder Stand from a very strong kick. *The position is held for four canter strides.*

The dismount may be made by: (1) returning to the Riding Seat and performing a simple Vault-off to the Inside; (2) performing a Half-Flank to the Inside or Outside; (3) coming down directly from the Shoulder Stand to the ground on the inside; (4) executing a Scissors in the air while coming down and returning to the Riding Seat facing backward, followed by Vault-off over the Croup, or by the alternative Flip-off described after the Scissors Vault-on.

A further variation is to perform the Shoulder Stand on the right side of the horse and finish with a somersault-off to the outside.

Caution: A somersault-off to the *inside* would be dangerous, as the youngster could get fouled in the longe line.

As with the Cossack Hang, practice the Shoulder Stand first at a standstill, and progress through the gaits.

ADVANCED WORK

Free Flank, or Flank-Over

The Free Flank is not mastered by all youngsters, but when done correctly it is very spectacular, especially when performed by several vaulters right behind each other — one coming up, one in the air, and one coming off!

The vaulter springs off the ground with great energy, legs together and stretched straight with toes pointed. With strongly pushing arms and shoulders to attain as much body elevation as possible, he swings the entire body completely over the back of the horse without touching the horse with any part of his body, landing on the right, or off, side, well away from the horse.

Many boys can do this Flank-Over beautifully, but most girls do not have the strength and push in their arms and shoulders to clear the back of the horse — they can get over the horse, but not without touching it.

Vault-off over the Croup

Out of the Riding Seat facing backward the vaulter places his hands on each side of the root of the tail. The upper body bends forward, arms pressing strongly, while the legs are swung fairly high behind and kept wide apart so they will come down on each side of the croup to the ground. The push-off is made when the croup is elevated by the horse's inner hind foot leaving the ground, giving added impetus to the spring. The vaulter must keep his weight forward as he comes off so that, if he should stumble, he will fall forward away from the horse's feet.

In this Vault-off over the Croup he has pushed off well and will land in good forward balance.

ADVANCED WORK

Reverse Flag

The Reverse Flag can be developed out of the normal Flag (see "The Six Compulsory Exercises") in the following manner.

After performing the ordinary Flag, the vaulter returns to the Half-Flag (leg still extended, but hands on grips) and swings his outstretched right leg energetically to the right, taking the weight on the arms and turning the body to the right, landing astride the neck of the horse *in front of the surcingle,* facing backward. He quickly brings his left leg into support across the neck of the horse and again comes into the full Flag position.

Roll-up

The Roll-up is an especially exciting *Kür* exercise. Since it is begun from the Riding Seat facing the rear of the horse, the vaulter may perform either the Scissors from the Riding Seat, or do the Scissors Vault-on. Still holding on to the grips, he pushes himself farther toward the tail until he can lie down flat on his back and change his hand-grip position, sliding his hands through the grips, palms up. He then stretches out full length, his arms straight, legs hanging over the croup of the horse. Swinging both legs up over his head, he does a back somersault to land seated on the neck in front of the surcingle, facing backward.

Caution: The vaulter must keep his legs well spread during the somersault so that his feet will neither slip *in-*

SINGLE KÜR EXERCISES

side the side reins nor hit the side reins, giving the horse a painful blow in the mouth.

From the position on the neck facing the rear, hands holding the grips, the vaulter may either:

(1) Do a Flip-off by swinging the right leg high over the neck of the horse, turning his body right, landing on the ground on the outside at the shoulder of the horse, facing forward.

Or (2) he could come into the Reverse Half-Flag by placing his left leg across the neck of the horse, extending his right leg high and straight. Keeping his right leg straight, the vaulter swings it energetically to the right, taking his full weight on his arms and turning his body with the leg, ending up in the normal Riding Seat facing forward.

A very spectacular and difficult exercise is the Reverse Half-Flag directly out of the Roll-up. As the vaulter is turning over in the somersault, he bends his left leg, knee out, so that his leg will be across the neck of the horse as he finishes the somersault and then pushes himself on up into the Half-Flag position. The key to success in this exercise is getting the left leg sufficiently bent during the somersault so that it will be firmly across the neck of the horse as the vaulter comes out of the somersault, and not just slip down on the side of the neck.

* * *

Many other attractive and spectacular individual performances can be made up by putting together several exercises. One good example would be a Vault-on into Side Seat to the Inside, followed immediately by a Three-quarter Scissors, and finished with a Flip-off.

ADVANCED WORK

COMBINED KÜR EXERCISES

Using all the exercises for individual vaulters heretofore described, there are endless combinations which can be worked out using two or three vaulters or more — three being considered the maximum to use in fairness to the horse, and this number only if it is a very strong horse and the vaulters not too heavy. Exercises by more than one vaulter are used in the Kür portion of competitions and also form the high points of exhibitions.

The number of possible combinations is limited only by the imagination and ingenuity of the instructor and the children. We will describe and picture some of those most commonly practiced, which will give some ideas with which to start.

Method of Mounting

We will begin with the method by which the second vaulter (or third) mounts the horse, shown in part in the photograph.

After the first youngster has vaulted on, he holds the right surcingle grip firmly with his *left* hand, at the same time passing his right arm behind his back to offer the right hand to the second youngster. The second youngster canters alongside holding onto the left surcingle grip with the left hand. He then grasps the mounted child's right wrist firmly with his right hand (the mounted vaulter also using the wrist-grip). The two count three canter strides together and *on the third,* the second vaulter pushes off from both feet and, with the pulling help of the mounted child, is brought into the Riding

KÜR COMBINATIONS

Seat behind him. When the second vaulter is learning, or with a small child to be brought up, the seated vaulter can give an assisting boost with his left leg quite effectively.

This is the correct position for vaulters' hands and wrist-to-wrist grip for taking up another vaulter. Note how the seated vaulter holds on to the right grip with her left hand to counterbalance the weight of the mounting vaulter, who will use the left grip to help spring up behind.

In this Kür combination of Flag and Reverse Flag, the vaulters' right legs are well aligned, but ideally they would stretch their left arms forward in full Flag, not this half-Flag, position.

KÜR COMBINATIONS

Double Flag

If the youngsters are not the same size, for the Double Flag the first vaulter-up should be the smaller one. He holds the grips as far down as possible so that the youngster behind can take hold of them at the top. Both youngsters kneel and place their left legs to the right across the horse's back. *They count together to three,* and then both stretch their right legs to the rear, straight and high with toes pointed. By counting again they can stretch their left arms forward.

Because of the low position of his hands, the youngster in front will make the Flag with his leg lower than the rear youngster's. Also, he should place his body forward so that his waist almost comes over his hands. This allows the second vaulter to bring his arms down to the grips at the waistline of the first youngster, the narrowest point of the body for him to span.

The beauty of this exercise is in the parallel placement of the vaulters' right legs and the rhythmic swinging of the legs with the horse's canter, as well as the parallel placement of the left arms, if they are outstretched.

The Double Flag can also be very pretty when done with the second vaulter standing, supported by his right arm on the back, close to the neck of the kneeling vaulter in front. In order to give adequate and firm support to the standing vaulter, the youngster kneeling must keep his supporting arms straight and rigid. The standing youngster must keep his weight strongly over his right arm, or he will overbalance to the inside and come off.

A spectacular variation is for the front vaulter to perform the Flag facing the rear of the horse, his supporting left leg on the neck of the horse, while the second youngster does the normal Flag facing forward.

ADVANCED WORK

The Arabesque with a beautifully stretched leg. The strength of the boy as the base makes it possible for the girl to achieve graceful lines and hold the position steadily and long for its full effect.

KÜR COMBINATIONS

Arabesque

In the Arabesque the front vaulter sits, the rear vaulter stands. The standing youngster is supported by holding on to the seated vaulter's wrists, which are out to the side and overhead, as shown in the photograph. The standing vaulter leans forward and finds balance on the left foot, while extending the right leg straight back and as high as possible. This is not an easy exercise.

Slightly harder is the shoulder-kneeling variation,

Good elevation and stretch in this kneeling Arabesque, but it would be helped if the second base vaulter had put her hands on the waist of the front base for support, and not pushed forward to hold the grips. With a small youngster behind, this exercise can also be performed by standing on the left shoulder of the base.

ADVANCED WORK

where a small standing vaulter places his left knee on the left shoulder of a strong, seated vaulter and stretches the right leg to the rear. The exercise is made easier all round if two seated vaulters are used, and the knee is supported by both shoulders.

Double Cross

The Double Cross is perhaps the simplest combination, but nonetheless it is pretty when well done.

The first vaulter remains in the Riding Seat, the second youngster coming to his knees behind him. Then both vaulters hold their arms out straight from their shoulders, palms down, fingers together, with good posture, eyes forward, arms slightly higher than the shoulders. Four strides are enough, although this combination is so easy that it can be held for several strides longer.

Slightly more difficult variations are to have the second youngster stand instead of kneel, or to have the first vaulter kneel and the second one stand.

Jump-Through

With a strong youngster sitting in front and a small, light youngster behind, the Jump-Through is spectacular.

The smaller vaulter behind stands and is supported by the hands of the seated youngster, as for the Arabesque. At the count of three, the rear vaulter jumps energetically high with strong pressure on the arms of the seated vaulter, and, with knees drawn up as high as possible, jumps over the head of the seated vaulter to land

In the Jump-Through the jumper can land seated or standing in front of the surcingle, or can go clear down to the ground on the outside. A second later, the girl stretched out her legs (toes pointed!) to avoid tangling with the side reins.

either seated or standing on the neck of the horse just in front of the surcingle.

Caution: If landing seated, great care must be taken that the jumping vaulter spreads his legs sufficiently so as not to catch on the side reins and give the horse a blow in the mouth.

One variation is for the youngster behind to jump over the right shoulder of the seated vaulter, landing on his feet on the ground on the right side of the horse.

A second variation is to have two seated vaulters, the third youngster jumping over both and through the arms of the first vaulter.

ADVANCED WORK

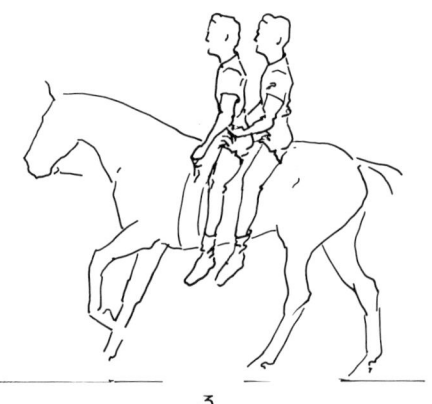

Figure 12. The Transfer

KÜR COMBINATIONS

The Transfer

The Transfer is an effective and very useful combination exercise which is not difficult to learn, but quite difficult to describe. The essence of it is that the youngster seated in front is swung around by the second vaulter to come into the Riding Seat behind him (Figure 12).

There are several ways the Transfer can be effected, depending upon the size and strength of the youngsters, as well as their experience with the exercise. The more experienced they are, the more they simplify the method. The following procedure is recommended for youngsters of equal size and strength.

The front vaulter to be transferred sits in side position to the inside on the neck of the horse *in front of the surcingle,* turned toward the rear of the horse with his left leg across the left leg of the second vaulter, who is in the normal Riding Seat. With his left arm, the front vaulter holds firmly around the second youngster's right hip, holding on to the mane with his right hand. The second vaulter, holding the right grip with his right hand, places his left arm across the front youngster's back, his hand reaching toward the right hip (as in Step 1). *At the count of three,* the first youngster pushes off, swinging his right leg over the horse's back behind the second vaulter (Step 2), grasping him around the waist with his right arm — while at the same moment the second youngster's left arm adds impetus and support to the swing in a scooping motion. With much practice, a courageous youngster in front position needs very little help from the second vaulter.

ADVANCED WORK

Flag and Cossack Hang

When these exercises are combined by two vaulters, the one in front performs the Cossack Hang while the second youngster performs the Half- or full Flag, as in the photograph.

The second youngster waits for the first to come into side-seat position to the right before coming to his knees (the first vaulter would have already placed his right foot in the loop when he first got on). As the front vaulter swings down into the Hang, the second youngster extends his right leg, and the Flag is completed by the second youngster extending his left arm. *The positions are held for four strides.*

Other variations are: (1) Double Cossack Hang (one on each side); (2) Cossack Hang with the second vaulter standing; (3) Double Cossack Hang with a third vaulter doing a Flag, Shoulder Stand, or a Stand after the other two are hanging down.

Too much bend in "flag's" knee and "cossack's" arms was corrected a moment later in this Flag and Cossack Hang.

KÜR COMBINATIONS

The two vaulters are well matched in size — an imperative in making the Double Cossack Hang a harmonious combination — and their legs are well stretched and aligned.

ADVANCED WORK

Wheelbarrow

The Wheelbarrow takes much practice.

First, both youngsters come to the Kneel and then the second vaulter does the Stand. Immediately the kneeling youngster — supporting himself firmly on his arms — gives the standing youngster first his right leg held firmly straight, toe pointed, then the left leg. *The position is held for four strides.*

It is very spectacular when an experienced vaulter (in the front position) can kick up into the Wheelbarrow with one energetic swing.

The youngsters can come out of this combination in several ways:

The standing vaulter simply lets go, and the "wheelbarrow" returns to a seated position.

Or the standing vaulter can push the legs of the "wheelbarrow" up and forward, the front vaulter dropping down onto his shoulder into a Shoulder Stand. The standing vaulter then pushes both legs of the "wheelbarrow" toward the outside and the front vaulter drops to the ground.

Supported Handstand

In the Supported Handstand, the vaulter who will do the handstand comes to a standing position behind the first vaulter in the Riding Seat, and leans forward over the seated vaulter to take hold of the surcingle grips. The seated vaulter grasps him at the waist and helps him come into the Handstand, where he remains holding the grips, his arms firm and straight, while continuing to be supported at the hips by the seated vaulter.

KÜR COMBINATIONS

A variation is to have the supporting vaulter stand and render support by holding the ankles of the one doing the Handstand. This variation is developed out of the Wheelbarrow.

Here the "wheelbarrow" has kicked up from a seated position, thus helping the standing vaulter to maintain his balance, plus making a smoother exercise. Good form throughout.

ADVANCED WORK

Stand and Shoulder Stand

In the combined Stand and Shoulder Stand, shown in the photograph, the youngster seated in front performs the Shoulder Stand.

First he leans forward to allow the rear vaulter to perform the Stand; he then comes quickly to his knees and into the Shoulder Stand. As his feet come up, the standing vaulter grasps them and holds him in a nice straight Shoulder Stand *for four strides.*

To come down from this position, the front vaulter brings a leg down on each side of the standing vaulter, and both return to the Riding Seat.

Or the standing vaulter may push the shoulder-standing front vaulter's legs to the outside, and the front vaulter then drops to the ground, as described under the variations of the Wheelbarrow.

The Stand and Shoulder Stand well done. It can be developed easily from the Wheelbarrow.

KÜR COMBINATIONS

Side view of a Double-Decker in which the top vaulter, a bit careless, has not hooked her toes securely enough around the base's back (a lapse due to overconfidence).

Double-Decker

The Double-Decker is developed by one vaulter in the Riding Seat (front) and one performing a Stand (behind). The standing youngster, holding on to the chin of the seated vaulter, puts first one and then the other leg over the shoulders of the seated vaulter. The legs then go under the arms of the seated vaulter with the toes hooked behind his back, as seen in the side-view photograph. When the top youngster is firmly seated on the shoulders of the one underneath, with toes locked in place, both extend their arms straight out to the side (see front, overleaf).

ADVANCED WORK

This Double-Decker shows clearly the need for paying attention to even the smallest details in combination work to ensure complete harmony of line: the girl's left arm and hand are slightly rotated and not fully stretched.

KÜR COMBINATIONS

The Bridge (see also overleaf) is not difficult, and in good form like this is always effective.

ADVANCED WORK

The Bridge

The Bridge is developed in the same manner as the Double-Decker, except that instead of hooking the legs around the seated vaulter, the second vaulter puts his toes under the grips of the surcingle, assisted by the seated vaulter. Slowly he leans back over the shoulders of the seated vaulter until he can put his outstretched fingertips on each side of the horse's back, gaining added support. The seated youngster may put his feet in the cossack-hang loops of the surcingle if he needs additional support. When the Bridge is in place, the seated vaulter stretches his arms out straight to the side.

Flying Angel

The Flying Angel is a spectacular and comparatively easy combination for three vaulters — two strong ones and one very small youngster. The two stronger ones mount first and bring the smaller child up behind them. The small vaulter stands up and leans far enough over the vaulter seated directly in front of him to allow the *front* vaulter to grasp him under his shoulders. At the same time the vaulter seated behind grasps the "angel" by the hips, and together the two seated vaulters support the smaller one over their heads in a horizontal "flying" position — arms outstretched to the side, body straight, legs together, toes pointed, head up.

*   *   *

KÜR COMBINATIONS

The Flying Angel in excellent form, except that the "angel's" arms could be more out to the side in a flying position.

ADVANCED WORK

The same Flying Angel, to emphasize the security in its execution. The "angel" is being supported correctly — behind the armpits and at the hips — and is comfortable and confident, while the bases are well aligned.

KÜR COMBINATIONS

Special Note to Instructors

Even while reading the descriptions and studying the photographs and drawings, many other possibilities will occur to the imaginative instructor. No attempt has been made to describe all of the combinations seen in competition today, since so much depends upon the skill of the instructor, the strength and disposition of the horse, and the courage of the youngsters.

Build slowly and carefully in order to encourage the youngsters, and use good judgment in pairing them for the various combined exercises. The strong and courageous ones can do much to develop the confidence of the more timid ones.

In preparing combinations for competition and exhibitions, try to group exercises which can develop out of each other smoothly. Thus, two or three youngsters can do several exercises without dismounting and without time-consuming changes in preparatory positions. This gives a much more fluid and attractive picture than when the children are constantly jumping on and off to perform just one exercise at a time.

For competitive teams, a translation of a German competition specification, together with the official judging sheets from their National Rule Book, have been provided in the Appendix.

Exhibitions

Exhibitions are excellent stimuli for a vaulting group, bringing a renewed spark and interest to their work. Such exhibitions can take two forms: (1) a *demonstration* of the method and progression of the work, in which case youngsters of varying abilities would be used — with their attendant (and amusing) mistakes; or (2) a finished *showpiece,* in which case only the very best performers would be used in a first-class presentation. Interestingly enough, both types of exhibitions are well received, even by audiences who are seeing vaulting for the first time. Also, both types of exhibitions seem equally effective in attracting young newcomers to the sport.

The demonstration type of exhibition is much easier to prepare and to create an effective climax for. Audiences delight in seeing first the very small children just beginning, who may even perform at a trot rather than a canter. And if one or two little ones can be used in a couple of combination exercises where, with the help of the bigger vaulters, they are able to be brought up in to the Riding Seat, so much the better! From there, several

ENTRY AND EXIT

more finished exercises by the advanced vaulters nicely round out the demonstration.

For either type of exhibition, the entry and exit are very important and should be practiced diligently. The vaulting instructor leads, trotting at the left shoulder in step with the horse. The children follow immediately behind the horse, single file according to size, and they should all be in step with the instructor. In a basic entry, the children then form a line alongside the instructor on the left side of the horse and at a given signal, all bow. If there is to be an introduction at that point, all wait in line until it is finished. A basic exit would be done in the same manner. Many pleasing variations can be worked out in both entries and exits.

Entry of a demonstration team — in step with the horse?

EXHIBITIONS

Line-up of the demonstration group (a competition team would have eight). *All vaulters should have held their arms the same — either at their sides or behind their backs.*

At a signal from the instructor, the vaulters move away to a predesignated point outside the circle the horse will make, and preferably facing the audience. After each exercise, the youngsters return to the line. It is also important for the picture as a whole that the children awaiting their turns stand in good posture, arms behind their backs or at their sides (in any event, all alike), and as quietly as is reasonably possible. While one vaulter is performing, the next youngster stands in the circle just behind the instructor. When it is his turn, the instructor lifts the longe whip high for the child to pass under. At that moment, the youngster must pick up the rhythm of the canter *on the left leg* and canter out along the longe line to the horse (or trot in step and in rhythm, if working at a trot). *The youngsters should*

IN THE RING

never take more than four strides alongside the horse before vaulting on.

For the demonstration type of exhibition, a commentary which has been carefully prepared for the show announcer — or preferably, given by someone who un-

For this finale the three mounted ones vaulted on over the croup. For full effectiveness the right shoulder of the kneeling vaulter should have been raised to align.

EXHIBITIONS

derstands what is going on — is an asset to the demonstration.

For the showpiece, no explanations are necessary, and a musical accompaniment adds a great deal to the presentation. Most shows have public address systems with which records can be played, and riding records are available for both the trot rhythm for the entry and the canter rhythm for the performance.

The children must be neatly turned out in matching dress.

The horse should be braided and bandaged to match the color of the children's outfits.

The instructor should be in formal riding dress—black coat, white breeches, black boots, and top hat or bowler.

* * *

Above all, do not forget there will be occasional mistakes and failures, but if the children are taught to accept them with good humor and a smile, the audience will be pleased too. Such occasional failures serve to point up the difficulties involved! If an exercise misfires, the child or children should repeat it, but only *once,* whether it then succeeds or not.

The charm of the performance will be in the obvious happiness, relaxation and spirited participation of the group. This precious spirit must be built into the group by the understanding, enthusiasm, good humor, and good judgment of the vaulting instructor, who spells the difference between the success and failure of any vaulting club.

Competitions

Competitive vaulting between teams of youngsters is a long-established sport in Germany and the rules covering it are contained in a National Rule Book. The specifications and judging sheet to be found in the Appendix reflect most of these rules. Following are a few of the main points.

GERMAN SPECIFICATIONS

Teams consist of eight children. Competitions may be "open" as to age, or may be limited to certain age groups. They may also be limited to nonwinners or nonplacers.

Every child on a team must perform all six of the Compulsory Exercises and is individually scored on each. Every child must participate in the Kür.

All work must be done on the cantering horse, and only exercises performed at a canter are scored. Each exercise must be sustained for four strides.

Each team is given 15 minutes to make its entire presentation of the Six Compulsory Exercises *(Pflicht)* and the Kür. It is estimated that the Compulsory Exercises require 8 to 10 minutes, leaving 5 to 7 minutes for the Kür. Competition may specify 10 minutes for the Compulsory and 5 minutes for the Kür.

COMPETITIONS

Certain conditions are sometimes added that are not on the official judging sheet. For small youngsters performing the Stand, use of the standing rein may be permitted. For older, more experienced vaulters, the Free Vault-off may be required; a better score is given if it is used.

MODIFICATIONS

Since there is a great deal of value in holding little competitions between groups even before the youngsters have become as proficient as the official rules require, we have found it very satisfactory to adopt some special modifications of our own, as follows.

If groups do not have eight vaulters, they can agree on a smaller number of contestants. All the teams need not even have the same number, as the scores are averaged.

Since 15 minutes is a very long time for a horse to sustain a canter, we have found that it works very well to have the teams perform the Compulsory Exercises alternately, e.g., one team goes out and each member does the Vault-on into the Riding Seat. Then the team retires to the sidelines and the next team performs the same exercise, etc. Not only does this procedure save the horse, but it makes the comparison of the teams' work much more interesting to the audience and to the teams themselves. When the Compulsory Exercises have been completed, each team performs a 3- to 5-minute *Kür* in its entirety.

It has also been found that it takes a long time before

SPECIFICATIONS

all youngsters can proficiently perform all exercises at the canter. Some very small children may even have to work at the walk in doing the more difficult exercises. Co-efficients are therefore used in scoring. If the child performs an exercise at the walk, he receives his score of from 0 to 10; if at a trot, his score is multiplied by 2; and if at a canter, multiplied by 3.

If a required exercise is unsuccessful, the child can repeat it *once,* but automatically loses half the points.

If the horse does not remain at a canter throughout the performance of an exercise, the child is credited for performing at a trot only. The horse is, of course, permitted to trot between contestants. The judge may use his discretion about a momentary break in gait.

The exercise is scored "Insufficient" if the vaulter does not perform the correct vault-off for a Compulsory Exercise.

The child is required to vault on within four strides after taking the surcingle grips. The exercise has to be started within four strides after coming into the Riding Seat. If the exercise has more than one part (Kneeling and Flag, Scissors), each part has to be commenced within four strides after finishing the preceding part.

KÜR SPECIFICATIONS

Exercises can be composed of singles not performed in the Compulsory routine, as well as combinations with two or more vaulters.

COMPETITIONS

JUDGING

It can readily be seen that for some time, a major difficulty in holding competitions will be the lack of knowledgeable judges. They will have to be trained and grow with the sport. Therefore, it is quite necessary at first to spell out in considerable detail just what is to be scored and what is to be penalized.

Judging a vaulting competition presents as many problems and is as demanding as dressage judging. In the Compulsory part of the competition, the judge must evaluate each youngster's performance of the six exercises with a score from 0 to 10. Some of the exercises take only about 10 seconds to perform, from vault-on to vault-off. The judge must be ready to give a numerical evaluation of this performance almost at the moment that the vaulter touches the ground at the finish, because another youngster will be instantly vaulting on.

The Phases

To make things even more difficult, the exercise actually breaks itself down into three phases — the vault-on, which must be correct; the performance of the exercise itself; and the vault-off, which must not only be properly performed, but also must be the correct one for that particular exercise. It also must be noted whether the exercise was begun within the required number of strides, was held for the required four strides, and whether there were any breaks in gait by the horse.

JUDGING

The Basics

The three basics which must be present in all exercises are *Rhythm,* form, and grace, in that order. Rhythm must be apparent in everything the vaulter does — his approach to the horse (in step), vault-on in rhythm with the horse, the performance of the exercise in rhythm with the horse, and the vault-off. When the rhythm requirement is met, then good form must be demonstrated throughout — straightness of legs; pointed toes; legs together; alignment of body, legs and arms; elevation. And all must be done with grace — harmonious, elegant suppleness.

Essence of the "Compulsories"

The judge must have a knowledge of the *essence* of each exercise, as well as understanding its difficulties and its beauties. For instance, the essence of the Mill is the rhythm of the exercise — that the vaulter moves his legs in an *exact* count. It is easy to do the Mill if the vaulter may move his legs whenever he pleases. If he does not move his legs on an exact count, no matter how good his form and elevation are, he could not receive a score of more than 4.

The essence of the Riding Seat is a supple back and balanced seat. The difficulties are to keep the legs stretched with toes pointed, the arms at slightly higher than shoulder level and straight from the shoulders, not "swept back."

The essence of the Flag is the harmonious alignment

of the outstretched leg and arm. The difficulties are sufficient elevation of a straight right leg and the sustaining of balance between the left knee and supporting right arm for four strides.

The essence of the Flank is the perfect rhythm in the changes from one side to the other while attaining maximum elevation of the legs in the kicks. The difficulties are to attain the elevation and to keep the legs absolutely together and straight in both changes.

The essence of the Stand is the very slightly bent knees moving supplely with the horse. The difficulties are the retention of balance while keeping the back straight, the arms stretched at slightly higher than shoulder level, straight out from the shoulders without being swept back, and only slightly bending the knees.

The essence of the Scissors is the perfect timing of the two changes, in rhythm with the horse's canter, while attaining maximum elevation in both changes. The difficulties are to make both changes with elegance and grace, characterized by making the changes as slow as possible, keeping the legs absolutely straight, with toes pointed, and landing exactly centered on the horse's back in both changes.

The Clerk

The judge should have a clerk to write in the scores as he gives them, so he does not have to take his eyes from the action. The clerk should be familiar enough with the sport and alert enough to handle the co-efficients, if they are to be used.

JUDGING

Aspects of the Kür

Judging the Kür also presents its difficulties, but the judge does have a little more time at the end in order to consider the two aspects to be scored: content and performance. In assessing the content of the program presented, he must take into account the variety of the program; the difficulty of the exercises which have been selected; the construction of the program — does it have a build-up to a finale?

In judging performance, the judge must consider care, control, and form throughout the presentation.

Note must be taken of any failure to perform attempted exercises. And finally, matters in which a knowledgeable clerk could be of great assistance, do all of the youngsters of the team participate?

The general impression score gives the judge the opportunity to evaluate with one score his feelings concerning the quality of: the entrance; the exit; the instructor; the horse; the dress; and the deportment and spirit of the group, which should be disciplined, enthusiastic and happy.

It should be kept in mind that it is not the purpose of classical vaulting to produce circus performers with breathtaking feats of derring-do. A simple program performed with grace and ease by confident children obviously enjoying themselves, would be far preferable to one containing very difficult exercises being hesitantly and stiffly carried out by tense, worried youngsters.

The use of more than one judge is recommended, not only to ensure more complete observation, but to afford the opportunity of bringing along more judges.

SUMMARY OF HINTS FOR VAULTING INSTRUCTORS

Practice Procedures

It is best to work on just one exercise or part of an exercise at a time with the entire group, letting each child try it once — or perhaps twice if he fails — and then on to the next. The exercise can be repeated over and over through the group until mastered by practically all, or until it is apparent that no more progress is likely at that particular time. This method ensures the continued attention of the entire group, because each vaulter must be alert and ready for his turn. By holding their undivided attention, the youngsters are able to learn faster because they will watch each other's efforts with more interest.

An order of going should be established and adhered to, and as one child vaults onto the horse, the next youngster should already be at the instructor's side ready to go next. This keeps the group on its toes and in good spirit. It also assures an economical use of the horse and maximum time for each child to practice.

As the children leave the instructor's side to vault on, they must always go under the instructor's raised whip. Doing this not only gives them a signal to go, but also puts them in a position to go out along the longe line, staying in line with the surcingle. In this way they have the shortest distance to cover; and they are not forced to chase the horse to catch up — not only very tiring, but possibly dangerous as well.

Do not allow the youngsters to hesitate endlessly to try an exercise while the horse goes round and round:

SUMMARY

insist that they try it or dismount. Then the problem can be analyzed further, and perhaps the hesitant ones should try it again at a slower gait or even a standstill.

Importance of Form

Insist upon good form at all times, even in the simplest things. Always legs straight, toes pointed, heads up, backs straight— all the elements of good posture. When arms are outstretched, they should be parallel with shoulders or a little higher, palms down, fingers closed, thumbs under. Insist that the vaulters keep their shoulders parallel with those of the horse at all times and most particularly in vaulting on and off.

When in the Riding Seat, the vaulter should be in good posture but relaxed, not stiff. Legs should hang down naturally, not held as if for riding with toes up.

Consideration for the Horse

Encourage the youngsters to bring cut-up carrots for the horse, but he should be fed only when so directed by the instructor.

Watch carefully that the children do not dig their toes into the back of the horse or their heels into the flanks. Do not allow them to flop down on his back with all their weight when doing Scissors, or returning to the Riding Seat from the Kneel or Stand. Teach them to take the weight on the arms. These precautions will preserve the good temper of the horse.

SUMMARY

Under no circumstances allow the child to kick or hit the horse to make it go on. All directions to the horse must be given by the instructor.

Check the surcingle occasionally for snugness. It is dangerous for the child if the surcingle slips, and it is very hard on the horse.

At the close of the session be sure that someone has been assigned to take care of the horse — sponge or rub the back and girth areas, and, if needed, to walk and rub the horse to cool him out.

Always check for possible signs of galling in the girth area after work, and take appropriate action at the first sign of trouble.

Glossary and Index

ARABESQUE: A Kür combination performed by two vaulters, in which a base vaulter supports by his wrists a vaulter standing behind him, the latter standing with his left leg in support and his right leg extended behind him.
68-70; ills. 68, 69

BASE: A term used to denote the seated vaulter in a Kür combination who supports and assists a second vaulter to perform an exercise.
64-84, with ills. passim

BIT-RING: The ring attached to each end of the bit to which the side reins are attached by a snap.
13; ills. 13 et seq.

BRIDGE: A Kür combination involving two vaulters — a base and a standing vaulter. The standing vaulter seats himself on the shoulders of the base, hooking his toes under the surcingle grips. He then leans back over the base's shoulders until he can touch the back of the horse with his hands.
81, 82; ill. 81

CAVESSON: A heavy bridle arrangement equipped with a padded metal noseband with a swivel ring on top into which the longe line is snapped, and an extra strap around the jaw to keep it from slipping on the horse's head. A cavesson is sometimes used for practice. (Instead, see Snaffle Bridle.)
12, 13, 114

COMBINATION: An exercise involving two or more vaulters.
64-85, with ills. passim

COMPULSORY DISMOUNTS: The particular dismount required for each of the Compulsory Exercises. The simple or free Vault-off is used for the first three compulsories; the fourth exercise (the Flank) uses the Half-Flank to the Outside; and the last two require the Half-Flank to the Inside (all q.v.).
21, 27, 44-48, 113, 114; ills. 45, 48

GLOSSARY AND INDEX

COMPULSORY EXERCISES: The six required individual exercises used in competitive vaulting: (1) Riding Seat, (2) Kneel and Flag, (3) the Mill, (4) the Flank, (5) the Stand, (6) the Scissors.
21, 27-48, 91, 95-96, 112-114; ills. 26-43 passim

COSSACK HANG: An individual Kür exercise in which the vaulter puts his right foot in the cossack loop on the off side of the surcingle and then hangs upside down toward the ground on the near side, arms over his head, left leg raised high.
24, 56-57, 74; ills. 57, 74

_____, **Double:** With a surcingle equipped with a cossack loop on both sides, two vaulters can perform the Cossack Hang, one hanging down on each side of the horse.
74-75; ill. 75

CROUP: That part of the horse's back between the top of the hip and the tail.
Ills. 18, 61

DISMOUNT: The finish of any vaulting exercise, and varies with the exercise (see Vault-off). For the Compulsories it is Vault-off to Inside for the Riding Seat, Kneel and Flag, and the Mill; Vault-off to Outside for the Flank (where in effect it is a Half-Flank to Outside); Half-Flank to Inside for the Stand and the Scissors.
See Compulsory Dismounts; Flip-off; Vault-off

DOUBLE CROSS: A Kür combination performed by two vaulters in which the first one is seated and the second kneels, or the first one kneels and the second stands.
Description, 70

DOUBLE-DECKER: A Kür combination performed by two vaulters, a base with another vaulter seated on his shoulders. Both have their arms stretched out horizontally.
79; ills. 79, 80

GLOSSARY AND INDEX

DOWNS-AND-UPS: A series of individual practice or *Kür* exercises in which the vaulter performs various vault-ons consecutively by dropping down to the ground and springing back on the horse in the same stride.
Description, 52

ELEVATION: The height achieved with the legs in making kicks. Maximum elevation is one of the hardest form requirements to master and is highly scored in competition.
22-23, 60, 95-96; ills. 23, 30, 37, 41, 46, 51, 54

FLAG: The second Compulsory Exercise in which the vaulter is supported on his left knee and right wrist, with the right leg stretched high and straight behind and the left arm stretched forward from the shoulder.
27, 31-32, 74, 95-96, 112, 113; ills. 30, 32, 66, 74

———, **Double:** A *Kür* combination performed by two vaulters, the base performing the Flag, the second standing on his left leg supported by his right arm on the right shoulder of the base, while he stretches his right leg out behind and his left arm forward, to match the arm and leg of the base.
Description, 67

———, **Half:** The rider supports himself on both wrists with his right leg stretched high and straight behind. The Half-Flag is performed by beginners only, before they can balance themselves for the full Flag.
31, 62; ill. 30

———, **Reverse:** An individual *Kür* exercise in which the Flag is performed facing backward, with the left knee across the neck of the horse. A *Kür* combination is often performed having one vaulter do the regular Flag while the second does the Reverse Flag on the neck at the same time.
62; ill. 66

———, **Reverse Half:** A Half-Flag (q.v.), but facing backward with the left knee on the neck of the horse. It can be part of an exciting individual *Kür* exercise in which it develops directly out of the Roll-up (q.v.).
Description, 63

GLOSSARY AND INDEX

FLANK: The fourth Compulsory Exercise, in which both legs are swung high behind and brought over together to the side seat to the inside. They are there swung together high over the back of the horse to the off side and the rider goes off the horse to the ground.
27, 36, 47, 96, 113; ill. 37

─────, **Half:** A form of vaulting off used in the last two Compulsory Exercises in which, from the Riding Seat, the vaulter swings both legs together high behind and brings them down together to the ground on the inside. It is also performed to the outside in *Kür* performances.
27, 38, 42, 47, 52, 59, 113, 114; ill. 46

FLANK-OVER: An individual *Kür* exercise in which the vaulter springs from the ground on the inside, carrying both legs over the back of the horse, to land on the ground on the outside.
Description, 60

FLIP-OFF: A dismount. *See* under Vault-off.
55, 63

FLYING ANGEL: A *Kür* combination involving three vaulters. Two bases support the third vaulter at the shoulders and hips in a horizontal "flying" position with his arms stretched to the sides and his legs straight out behind.
82; ills. 83, 84

GIRTH AREA: That part of the horse's belly on which the surcingle fastens.
100; ills. 13 et seq.

GRIPS: The two handles on the surcingle.
12-13; ills. 13 et seq.

HANDSTAND: A combination *Kür* exercise performed by two vaulters. The standing vaulter leans over the shoulders of the base, grasps the surcingle grips, and, supported by the base vaulter at the hips, comes up into a handstand.
76-77

GLOSSARY AND INDEX

JUMP-THROUGH: A Kür combination performed by two vaulters in which the standing vaulter jumps through the arms of the seated base, landing either on the withers of the horse or on the ground on the outside.
70-71; ill. 71

KICK: High kicks practiced by vaulters to improve form.
22-24; ills. 21, 41

KNEEL: Formerly part of the second Compulsory Exercise, where vaulter stretches up on his knees, arms held out to the sides.
27, 30-31, fn 112, fn 113; ill. 33

KÜR: A term taken from the German denoting the free-style portion of a vaulting competition.
27, 50-52, 56-84, 93, 97, 113, 114; ills. 51-84 passim

LEAPFROG: A warm-up exercise in which the vaulters space themselves in a line about 15 feet apart, and leaning over with heads down. Starting at the rear of the line, each vaulter in turn runs forward and vaults over each of the other youngsters in front of him, stopping 15 feet beyond the last child, where he, too, bends over. This exercise is used to develop spring and form.
17-18; ill. 18

LEG-UP: When small beginners cannot yet vault on, they are often given a leg-up in order that they may practice the exercises. A helper grasps the child's left knee and foot and, on counting three, tosses him up on the horse's back.

LONGE: To exercise or train the horse, or train the rider, while causing the horse to go on a circle around the trainer by means of a long line attached to a cavesson or bridle.
12-13, 16, 114; ills. 13, 20, 33 et seq.

————— **Line:** A webbing or nylon tape about 1½ inches wide and some 25 feet long, fastened to a cavesson or bridle and held in the trainer's hand, through which he controls the horse moving on a circle around him.

GLOSSARY AND INDEX

———— Whip: A whip with a lash long enough to reach the horse at the end of the longe line, used by the trainer to urge on the horse.
12, 19, 88, 114

MILL: The third Compulsory Exercise in which the vaulter turns completely around on the back of the horse by swinging one leg at a time over the neck or back of the horse, the legs being moved to an exact count with the stride of the horse.
27, 34, 95, 113; ill. 35

NEAR SIDE: The left side of the horse, from the rider's or vaulter's viewpoint (see Off Side).

OFF SIDE: The right side of the horse, from the rider's or vaulter's viewpoint (see Near Side).

PFLICHT: The German term for the Compulsory Exercises of a vaulting competition.
27, 115; see also Compulsory Exercises, Dismounts

REIN, Side: One of a pair of reins, one end of which is buckled to the rings on the sides of the surcingle and the other is snapped to the bit-ring of the bridle. Side reins are used to keep the horse's neck straight and his head down in position.
12, 114; ill. 13

————, Stand-up: The belt-like strap fastened to the ring on top of the surcingle which the beginning vaulters use in order to steady themselves in standing up on the horse.

RIDING SEAT: The first of the Compulsory Exercises in which the vaulter sits astride, facing forward, with arms outstretched to the side.
27-29, 30-79 passim, 95, 112, 113; ills. 26, 29, 33

ROLL-UP: An individual *Kür* exercise in which the vaulter, from a prone position on the horse's back, performs a backward somersault, ending up in front of the surcingle facing backward, or in a Reverse Flag on the neck of the horse.
62-63

GLOSSARY AND INDEX

SCISSORS: The sixth Compulsory Exercise in which, from the Riding Seat, the vaulter swings both legs high behind and crosses his legs so that he comes into the astride position again, facing the rear. He then swings both legs high up in front of him and crosses his legs, to bring him once more into the Riding Seat facing forward.
24, 27, 40-43, 52, 59, 96, 113, 114; ills. 41, 43

_____ **On:** A form of vault-on used in Kür exercises (see under Vault-on).
52, 53, 55; ill. 54

_____ **Off:** A form of vault-off used in Kür exercises (see under Vault-off).

_____, **Three-quarter:** An exercise begun from the side seat to the inside, in which the vaulter makes a three-quarter turn to the right, ending up astride, facing the croup.
50; ill. 51

SHOULDER STAND: An individual Kür exercise where the vaulter performs a shoulder stand on the neck of the horse just in front of the surcingle.
59, 78; ills. 58, 78

SIDE SEAT: A vaulter's position in which he is seated with both legs on the same side of the horse.
34, 36, 49, 50, 52

SIDE-TO-SIDE: A form exercise in which the vaulter practices swinging both legs from one side of the horse to the other.
Description, 49

SNAFFLE BRIDLE: Headgear for guiding or restraining the horse comprised of a headstall, snaffle bit, reins, throatlash, etc. Illustrations in the text show the longe line run over the horse's head in the French manner, rather than fastened to a cavesson (q.v.).
12, 13, 114; ills. 13, et seq.

GLOSSARY AND INDEX

STAND: The fifth Compulsory Exercise in which the vaulter comes from the Riding Seat to his knees and then to his feet, or directly from the Riding Seat to his feet, and stands with his arms held out straight to the side.
24, 27, 38, 52, 78, 96, 113, 114; ills. 39, 78

SURCINGLE: The vaulting surcingle is a leather girth which is buckled around the horse, fitted with two, preferably stiff, leather handles or grips; metal rings to which are attached side reins; a strap fastened to a ring on top called the stand-up rein to assist the beginners in standing; a leather loop on the off side (or one on each side) in which to insert the foot to perform the Cossack Hang.
12, 114, 115; ills. 13 et seq.

THROATLASH: The strap buckled under the horse's jaws to keep the bridle or cavesson from being pulled over the ears. This strap is always fitted loosely to allow the horse to flex easily.
12; ill. 13

TRANSFER: A Kür exercise for two vaulters in which the one seated in front is transferred to the rear.
72, 73; ill. 72

VAULTING (or Voltigieren or Voltige): Gymnastics on the back of the moving horse.

VAULT-OFF: One of various means of dismounting or finishing the Compulsory or Kür exercises.
27, 34, 38, 44-52, 59-60, 63, 71, 76, 78, 93, 94, 112-114;
ills. 45, 46, 61

———— **Flip-off:** Used in Kür exercises when the vaulter is sitting astride, facing the rear. The left leg is brought over the neck of the horse and the vaulter lands facing forward on the inside. When the vaulter is seated in front of the surcingle, he brings his right leg over, landing on the outside in order to avoid getting fouled in the longe line.
55, 63

GLOSSARY AND INDEX

———, **Free:** Used in place of the simple Vault-off to Inside (q.v.) for the first three Compulsory Exercises. Without holding the grips, the right leg is brought over the neck of the horse and the rider slides down to the ground, facing forward.
48, 92

———, **Half-Flank:** To inside, used for the fifth and sixth Compulsory Exercises, as well as for many Kür exercises. See Half-Flank under Flank.
27, 38, 42, 47, 59; ill. 46

———, **to Outside:** Used for the fourth Compulsory Exercise (the Flank) where it is part of the continuous motion of the exercise and thus can be considered a Half-Flank to Outside. The vaulter comes down on the right side of the horse, facing forward close to the horse.
27, 47, 59, 113, 114

———**Over the Croup:** Used in the Kür. When facing backward, the vaulter gives a high, leapfrogging push-off, to land on the ground with his back to the horse.
60; ill. 61

———, **Scissors:** Used in Kür exercises when the vaulter is facing the rear of the horse. By means of a high scissors kick, the vaulter leaps off to the ground, over the croup of the horse.

———, **Simple (to Inside):** Used in the first three Compulsory Exercises. The right leg is brought over the neck of the horse, and the rider slides down to the ground, facing forward, still holding the grips of the surcingle (if he is big enough).
21, 27, 34, 44, 59, 113, 114; ill. 45

VAULT-ON: The spring from the ground to get onto the back of the horse.
15, 19, 21, 27, 28-29, 36, 53-55; ills. 18, 20, 29

——— **Over the Croup:** A practice exercise with the standing horse to develop spring. The vaulters run from the rear of the horse and spring over the croup into the Riding Seat.
18, 89; ill. 18

GLOSSARY AND INDEX

———— **Scissors-on:** Used in *Kür* exercises. The vaulter swings his left leg to the rear over the croup of the horse, turning his body to the left and landing on the back of the horse, facing backwards.
53, 55; ill. 54

———— **Side Seat to Inside:** Used in *Kür* exercises. The vaulter springs directly into the side seat to the inside.
34, 53

———— **Side Seat to Outside:** Used in *Kür* exercises. Rider carries both legs across the back of the horse, to finish in the side seat to the outside.
34, 53, 55

———— **Simple (or Vault into the Riding Seat):** The basic vault-on used for all Compulsory Exercises and most of the *Kür* exercises. The right leg is raised over the back of the horse, the rider landing astride the horse, facing forward.
21, 27, 28-29; ills. 20, 29

WARM-UP, Horse: Preliminary exercising of the horse prior to vaulting to allow him to loosen up his muscles and relax his back. For the vaulting horse, it is a good idea to warm up to the right, since the vaulting will be done to the left.

————, **Children:** Ground exercises to get the children loosened up and thinking about good form. Recommended are tumbling, leapfrog, jumping back and forth over a low rope or the longe line held by two youngsters, etc.
17-18, 22, 48-52; ill. 18

WHEELBARROW: A *Kür* combination involving two vaulters. The rear vaulter stands and the front vaulter kicks up with his legs so that the standing vaulter can grasp them at the thighs and support him in this position.
76, 77, 78; ill. 77

GLOSSARY AND INDEX

WITHERS: The top of the horse's shoulderblades at the base of the neck top-line. The surcingle fits just behind the withers. The height of a horse is always measured from the top of the withers to the ground.

Appendix

SPECIFICATIONS FOR A VAULTING COMPETITION

(Translated directly from a German show classification)

GROUP A 12 years and younger.

GROUP B 16 years and younger.

GROUP C 16 years and younger, for children who have not yet been placed in a vaulting competition.

GROUP D 16 years and younger, for children who have not yet won a vaulting competition.

NUMBER OF CHILDREN: 8

EXERCISES FOR VAULTING COMPETITIONS

Compulsory Exercises

Group A — 12 years and younger

1. *Vault into the Riding Seat.* Arms at the sides. Vault-off to the Inside.

2. *Kneel* and Flag.* Vault-off to the Inside. It is optional whether both hands remain on the grips or the left arm is stretched forward. The outstretched right leg is compulsory.

   * The free Kneel is not required.

APPENDIX

3. *Mill.* Vault-off to the Inside.
4. *Flank.* Flank out of the Riding Seat.
5. *Stand.* Use of the standing rein permitted (it will, however, be evaluated). Stand at least four gallop strides. Glide into the Riding Seat. Vault-off to the Inside.
6. *Scissors.* Complete Scissors with return. Vault-off to the Inside. In the *Kür:* Vault-off to the Outside permitted.

Time for entire presentation, Compulsory Exercises 1–6 and *Kür* = 15 minutes.

Scoring:

Only that which is produced on the galloping horse will be scored. Obvious trotting: penalty points 0.5. For extreme breaks 1.0. These are to be added to the mark for Over-all Impression.

Marks:

0–10. To be evaluated: Compulsory Exercises 1–6, *Kür* exercises (x2). Over-all Impression of the group (x2).

Total = 10 individual marks. In the case of tie scores, changing of horses for the purpose of comparing groups is possible (5 min).

Group B — 16 years and younger

1. *Vault* into the Riding Seat. Arms at the sides. Vault-off to Inside.
2. *Kneel* and Flag.* Vault-off to Inside. The Flag is to be performed with forward-stretched left arm. The outstretched right leg is compulsory.
3. *Mill.* Vault-off to the Inside.
4. *Flank.* Free Flank or out of the side seat without first coming into the Riding Seat.

* The free Kneel is no longer required.

APPENDIX

5. *Stand.* Use of the standing rein permitted (it will, however, be evaluated). Stand at least four gallop strides. Glide into the Riding Seat. Vault-off to the Inside.

6. *Scissors.* Complete Scissors with return. Vault-off to the Inside. In the *Kür:* Vault-off to the Outside permitted.

Time for the entire presentation, Compulsory Exercises 1–6 and Kür = 15 minutes.

Scoring:

Only that which is produced on the galloping horse will be scored. Obvious trotting: penalty points 0.5. For extreme breaks 1.0. These are to be added to the mark for Over-all Impression.

Marks:

0–10. To be evaluated: Compulsory Exercises 1–6, Kür exercises (x2). Over-all Impression of the group (x2).

Total = 10 individual marks. In the case of tie scores, changing of horses for the purpose of comparing groups is possible (5 min).

THE VAULTING HORSE

Equipment: Vaulting surcingle. Snaffle with dropped noseband or cavesson noseband. Side reins. Bandages.
Pad or blanket not permitted for compulsory exercises and *Kür.* In exhibitions it is optional. No checkreins permitted.

Vaulting Teacher: Dress: White breeches, black coat, riding cap. Equipment: Longe, whip. Standing place in the circle is not to fluctuate!

Competitors: Maximum age: 16 years (Year of birth 19.. or younger).

APPENDIX

REFERENCES

Trick-Riding and Voltige by H. J. Lijsen and Antony Hippisley Coxe, J. A. Allen, 1 Lower Grosvenor Place, London. 1956.

Voltigieren by Dieter Schnelle. "Musterschmidt" Wissenschaftlicher Verlag, Gottingen, Germany. 1953 (in German).

Voltigieren Leicht Gemacht by Ursula Bruns. Albert Müller Verlag, Rüschlikon-Zurich. 1964 (in German).

Wir Voltigieren by Lorenz Kurz-Mönnig (in German).

Richtlinien für Reiten und Fahren, Band III — Richtlinien für das Voltigieren — Ponyreiten, — Reiterspiele. (Judges' handbook, in German). Available from: Hauptverband für Zucht und Prüfung deutscher Pferde e.V. — Deutsche Reiterliche Vereinigung (FN), 441 Warendorf i.W., Germany.

SOURCES FOR EQUIPMENT

There are undoubtedly many more, but with these we are familiar:

Vaulting Surcingles

G. Passier & Sohn, Am Pferdemarkt 8–10, 3012 Langenhagen / Hannover, Germany.

Books, Films, Riding Records

Dr. Rudolph Georgi, Wilhelmstrasse 90, 51 Aachen, Germany (send for catalog).

Films

Tiedemann-Film, Vahrenwalder Strasse 88, 3 Hannover, Germany:

Voltigieren, Pflicht- und Kürübungen (Vaulting, Compulsory and Kür Exercises). About 50 meters long. Black and white. 8mm or Super 8. About $15 for 8mm; 10% more for Super 8.

Kleine Reiter ganz gross, ein Voltigierfilm in Farbe. About 15 meters long. Color. About $8 for 8mm.

SCORING

NAME OF CLUB & VAULTING INSTRUCTOR	Contestant No.	REQUIRED EXERCISES					
		1 Riding Seat	2 Flag	3 Mill	4 Flank	5 Stand	6 Scissors
	1						
	2						
	3						
	4						
	5						
	6						
	7						
	8						
	TOTAL :8						
	1						
	2						
	3						
	4						
	5						
	6						
	7						
	8						
	TOTAL :8						
	1						
	2						
	3						
	4						
	5						
	6						
	7						
	8						
	TOTAL :8						

CHART

TOTAL	KÜR		General Im-pression	Total Points	P L A C E	CRITIQUE
	Content	Performance				
	×2	×2				
1-6	0-10	0-10	0-10	:11		

SCORING

NAME OF CLUB & VAULTING INSTRUCTOR	Contestant No.	REQUIRED EXERCISES					
		1 Riding Seat	2 Flag	3 Mill	4 Flank	5 Stand	6 Scissors
	1						
	2						
	3						
	4						
	5						
	6						
	7						
	8						
	TOTAL :8						
	1						
	2						
	3						
	4						
	5						
	6						
	7						
	8						
	TOTAL :8						
	1						
	2						
	3						
	4						
	5						
	6						
	7						
	8						
	TOTAL :8						

CHART

TOTAL	KÜR		General Im‐pression	Total Points	P L A C E	CRITIQUE
	Content	Performance				
1-6	×2 0-10	×2 0-10	0-10	:11		

SCORING

NAME OF CLUB & VAULTING INSTRUCTOR	Contestant No.	REQUIRED EXERCISES					
		1 Riding Seat	2 Flag	3 Mill	4 Flank	5 Stand	6 Scissors
	1						
	2						
	3						
	4						
	5						
	6						
	7						
	8						
	TOTAL :8						
	1						
	2						
	3						
	4						
	5						
	6						
	7						
	8						
	TOTAL :8						
	1						
	2						
	3						
	4						
	5						
	6						
	7						
	8						
	TOTAL :8						

CHART

TOTAL 1-6	KÜR		General Impression 0-10	Total Points :11	PLACE	CRITIQUE
	Content ×2 0-10	Performance ×2 0-10				

SCORING

NAME OF CLUB & VAULTING INSTRUCTOR	Contestant No.	REQUIRED EXERCISES					
		1 Riding Seat	2 Flag	3 Mill	4 Flank	5 Stand	6 Scissors
	1						
	2						
	3						
	4						
	5						
	6						
	7						
	8						
	TOTAL :8						
	1						
	2						
	3						
	4						
	5						
	6						
	7						
	8						
	TOTAL :8						
	1						
	2						
	3						
	4						
	5						
	6						
	7						
	8						
	TOTAL :8						

CHART

TOTAL 1-6	KÜR		General Impression 0-10	Total Points :11	PLACE	CRITIQUE
	Content ×2 0-10	Performance ×2 0-10				

SCORING

NAME OF CLUB & VAULTING INSTRUCTOR	Contestant No.	1 Riding Seat	2 Flag	3 Mill	4 Flank	5 Stand	6 Scissors
	1						
	2						
	3						
	4						
	5						
	6						
	7						
	8						
	TOTAL :8						
	1						
	2						
	3						
	4						
	5						
	6						
	7						
	8						
	TOTAL :8						
	1						
	2						
	3						
	4						
	5						
	6						
	7						
	8						
	TOTAL :8						

REQUIRED EXERCISES

CHART

TOTAL 1-6	KÜR		General Im-pression 0-10	Total Points :11	P L A C E	CRITIQUE
	Content ×2 0-10	Performance ×2 0-10				

SCORING

NAME OF CLUB & VAULTING INSTRUCTOR	Contestant No.	REQUIRED EXERCISES					
		1 Riding Seat	2 Flag	3 Mill	4 Flank	5 Stand	6 Scissors
	1						
	2						
	3						
	4						
	5						
	6						
	7						
	8						
	TOTAL :8						
	1						
	2						
	3						
	4						
	5						
	6						
	7						
	8						
	TOTAL :8						
	1						
	2						
	3						
	4						
	5						
	6						
	7						
	8						
	TOTAL :8						

CHART

TOTAL	KÜR		General Im-pression	Total Points	P L A C E	CRITIQUE
	Content	Performance				
1-6	×2 0-10	×2 0-10	0-10	:11		

Performance Record

SF
309
F86

Friedlaender, Elizabeth
Vaulting.

Rock Valley College